Libraries in the '80s:
Papers in Honor
of the Late Neal L. Edgar

About the Editor

DEAN H. KELLER is Assistant for Collection Development and Management at the Kent State University Library. He is a contributor to professional journals and the author of several books, including *An Index to Plays in Periodicals*.

Libraries in the '80s: Papers in Honor of the Late Neal L. Edgar

Dean H. Keller
Editor

The Haworth Press
New York • London

Libraries in the '80s: Papers in Honor of the Late Neal L. Edgar has also been published as *Technical Services Quarterly,* Volume 3, Numbers 1/2, Fall 1985/Winter 1985-86.

The Haworth Press, Inc., 28 East 22 Street, New York, NY 10010
EUROSPAN/Haworth, 3 Henrietta Street, London WC2E 8LU England

Library of Congress Cataloging in Publication Data
Main entry under title:

Libraries in the '80s.

  Includes bibliographic references index.
  1. Library science—Addresses, essays, lectures. 2. Libraries—Addresses, essays, lectures. 3. Edgar, Neal L., 1927- . I. Edgar, Neal L., 1927- . II. Keller, Dean H.
Z674.L463   1985   020   85-5862
ISBN 0-86656-459-4

Libraries in the '80s: Papers in Honor of the Late Neal L. Edgar

Technical Services Quarterly
Volume 3, Numbers 1/2

CONTENTS

Preface   ix

Friar Jerome and Brother Dominic   1
    Paul Z. DuBois

The Past Is Too Much With Us   9
    John P. Comaromi

The Sunny Book Review   17
    Bill Katz

Financing the Public Libraries of Ohio: A Problem
  in Resource Allocation   27
    A. Robert Rogers

QWL in Academic/Research Libraries   51
    Jean S. Decker

Commas, Colons, and Parentheses: The International
  Standardization of Serials Holdings Statements   59
    Marjorie E. Bloss

The Serials-Centered Library   73
    Barbara P. Pinzelik

Half of a Conversation With Neal Edgar   81
    Jean Acker Wright

Analysis of Monographic Series   85
    Ruth B. McBride

The Challenge of Educating Library and Information
    Science Professionals: 1985 and Beyond   97
    James E. Rush

''Give Peace A Chance'': Subject Access to Material
    on Nukes, Militarism, and War   113
    Sanford Berman

Authority Control: Issues and Answers   127
    Doris Hargrett Clack

Neal Lowndes Edgar 1927-1983   141
    Rosemary D. Harrick

Neal L. Edgar: A Bibliography of Professional Works   145
    Susan Barnard

Contributors   155

Preface

When we set out to gather essays for a festschrift in memory of Neal L. Edgar, our aim was to assemble a collection of widely diverse articles on librarianship, in its broadest sense, by an equally diverse group of contributors. Neal was like that. I know of no area of librarianship in which he did not have an interest, or in which he did not have knowledge, or in which he did not have an opinion.

The options available for contributions were many. Articles on cataloguing, serials, reference, *AACR2*, bibliography, indexing, the history of books and printing, and the philosophy of librarianship would have been appropriate. Neal wrote and thought about all of them. And the contributions need not to have been confined to library science, for Neal had a remarkably broad interest in scholarship in other areas, too.

The readers of the essays which follow will find that many of these topics have been addressed in a variety of ways. The practical, theoretical and philosophical approaches to books and libraries are all represented here.

Just as we looked for a great variety of subjects, and treatments of those subjects, for this collection, so it was that we tried to find contributors who had some relationship to Neal and who represented diverse aspects of librarianship. We were fortunate in finding people who had worked with Neal in libraries, especially at Kent State University, those who had known him in committee work in professional organizations, notably the American Library Association, those who found him to be an encouraging yet demanding editor, and those who knew him as a colleague in the teaching of library science. It was gratifying to have so many of Neal's friends come forward with contributions of such quality and diversity.

Anyone who knew Neal at all well knew he liked people. He constantly sought ideas and opinions, and, while he may not always have agreed with the idea or opinion, he could look beyond them to the person uttering them. Perhaps that is one reason why he had such a wide circle of friends and acquaintances. His generosity, encouragement, and assistance to those friends and acquaintances was extraordinary, and his support of younger colleagues and students remarkable. I venture to say that more than one of the contributors to this festschrift can attest to the help and advice Neal provided. Perhaps this willingness to listen, advise and encourage, and, very importantly, to criticize, is Neal's greatest legacy to our profession and to us individually.

Here, then, is our tribute to Neal Edgar, our friend and colleague. Even if our effort fails to encompass all that was in Neal's professional makeup, I somehow think he would approve, but not without some criticism, of course, of what is presented here.

It remains now for me to perform the pleasant task of acknowledging the help and encouragement I received from so many as I prepared this festschrift. First, I am grateful to all of the authors who so willingly and so effectively contributed to this book, for without them there could have been no book. Hyman W. Kritzer, former Director of the Kent State University Library, very generously suggested to Peter Gellatly, Senior Editor of The Haworth Press, Inc., that I might be the person to edit this book, and then Peter Gellatly was very generous with his advice, encouragement and patience as the book took shape. I appreciate the confidence of both of these gentlemen. Alberta Adolph and Judy Conley in the Director's office at the Kent State University Library were also helpful in a variety of important ways.

Finally, I am especially grateful to Susanna Edgar for believing that I knew Neal well enough to do justice to his memory as editor of this festschrift.

Dean H. Keller

Friar Jerome and Brother Dominic

Paul Z. DuBois

Friar Jerome, some readers will recall, was the hero of Thomas Bailey Aldrich's poem, "Friar Jerome's Beautiful Book." The Friar, out of penance for some half-imagined sin, devotes his life to illuminating the Gospels and as the years go by he creates a book that he hopes, in his forgivable pride, will be unsurpassed in its beauty. But then the plague strikes and Friar Jerome puts pride and his unfinished book aside to give succor to the sick and friendless. A broken and dying man, he finally returns to his book and it is then that he discovers that the Angel of God has finished his illuminations in colors and designs beyond the ken of any mortal. Aldrich's poem is sentimental and moralistic. Its underlying belief in sacrifice and in the inevitable links among work, service, beauty and knowledge strikes us today as quintessentially of the nineteenth century.

We are more comfortable with Brother Dominic in the 1980s—he of the Xerox (please to remember the capital X) commercials with his mischievous eyes and enterprising manner. Yes, there is still the illuminated leaf and there is still a voice of authority, this time demanding "500 copies," but the higher voice is not the voice of God but of Father Superior who suspiciously resembles a 20th century office manager. Is Brother Dominic shaken by the request? Not to worry. Brother Dominic waddles out of Father Superior's office back to his cell where he zaps the original leaf into a Xerox 1075 and Presto: 500 copies.

What a strangely effective advertisement that is justly worthy of the awards it has garnered. It speaks as an electronic 20th century icon to so many of the underlying assumptions of our time. There is the worship of speed, the fascination with medium over message, the boundless faith in technology and our amusement at the old notion that effort and accomplishment are related. Finally, of course, there is the subliminal message that religious figures are quaintly humorous, not to be taken seriously, unless like Brother Dominic they open their eyes to progress and install a 1075 in their own cells. Is this reading too much into a commercial? Perhaps, but Friar Jerome and Brother Dominic may stand without too much straining as representatives of the old and new librarianship.

Today in libraries we are all increasingly Brother Dominics. And since, as G.K. Chesterton once wrote, the strongest thing in any age is always too strong, it might be well to remind ourselves that Friar Jerome created with the help of God a beautiful book for the ages while Brother Dominic gives us only a batch of Xerox copies as perishable as last month's memoranda or next week's computer print-out.

Librarianship over the years has woven two strands together—the one a strand of human service that called for mind and spirit and had as one of its sacramental assumptions the notion that librarianship was more than just another way of making a living. It was a calling to enlighten the users of libraries, to inspire in them the passion for reading, to, in short, help people become all they are capable of becoming.

The other strand of librarianship was that characteristic American fascination with machinery and systems and management or "economy," elements which would help librarians to, in the hoariest of cliches, get the right book to the right reader at the right time. With the pioneers in the professionalization of librarianship, both strands were important. They were Yankee enterprisers, but they were also missionaries, and the notion that the humanistic thrust of librarianship could be separated from the technological would have been foreign, even pernicious, to them.

In short, librarianship in this country had from the beginning what the late E.F. Schumacher, author of *Small is Beautiful,* would call convergent and divergent elements to it. Schumacher's distinction is an important one and especially apt for librarianship. Convergent problems (How do you create an on-line catalog or an automated circulation system?) are those which each year finds us closer to solving as data accumulates and experiences are rationally analyzed. Such problems and their management offshoots are the issues discussed in over 90% of our literature, and those who deal with such problems have the immense advantage of knowing that they deal with soluble problems, with problems as Schumacher puts it that can be "killed."

Divergent problems are of a quite different sort, for here the answers do not come from the pursuit of straight line logic or the amassing of statistical data or even from the construction of cleverly designed questionnaires. Indeed, the more such problems are studied, the more the answers diverge rather than converge. Schumacher gives us a classic example of a divergent problem: the question of what is the best method of education. One answer suggests a structured environment where authority is recognized and where those who are ignorant learn from those who have knowledge. Another solution insists that freedom not obedience is at the heart of education and that once the resources are available the young should be free to select what they need without being required to follow another's direction. In the political sphere, a similar set of opposites involves the social goods of freedom and equality and how much each is to be encouraged at the expense of the other in a given society.[1]

Librarianship poses a host of divergent problems that resolve themselves if not into neat opposites at least into formulations that go beyond logic and quantification. Central to librarianship is a passion for reading and instilling that passion in others. Yet how airily idealistic this seems when the act of reading is still largely a mystery to us and when mere functional literacy is beyond the grasp of millions. There is the delicate matter of making the best in literature available to readers in an age when many would argue that the "best" is a purely subjective judgment that is only one step away from a subtle form of censorship. And once one strays into the thicket of censorship, there are the enormously complex challenges of defining obscenity and pornography, definitions which are now being informed by a feminist viewpoint largely ignored in earlier discussions.

I think all of these questions and a host of others are more than simply matters for pleasant speculation. The answers we reach as individuals and as a culture carry any number of practical implications. On the academic library level, we are still wrestling with the vital role of rare books in a college or university library and how that role is to be balanced with the more obvious utilitarian functions of the academic library. For those concerned with education for librarianship, there is the question of how to insure, in an era of managementese, that the humanistic roots and values of the profession will not be abandoned. How dreary so many of our library workshops have become with their parroting of the latest buzz words and concepts of management. How often the process, not the product,

becomes the message as librarians spend countless hours with goals
and objectives, cost-benefit analyses, evaluation forms—so much of
it destined for the mumbo-jumbo graveyard where zero-based budgeting and competency-based education now rest peacefully. Perhaps in taking a fresh look at some of the truly engaging questions of
librarianship we need to reflect on T.S. Eliot's words in the Choruses from "The Rock":

> Where is the Life we have lost in living?
> Where is the wisdom we have lost in knowledge?
> Where is the knowledge we have lost in information?[2]

I do not doubt that there may be some convergent elements in all
these divergent questions, but in essence they are living questions,
not questions ready to be killed by a piece of machinery or a technological system. As living questions involving paradoxes, they will
be struggled with and "solved" by men and women capable of unty-
ing paradoxes through the qualities that have always been associated
with the humanistic side of librarianship. . . . what Schumacher
calls the "faculties of a higher order . . . love, empathy, participation mystique, understanding, compassion."[3] These are among the
qualities Thoreau had in mind when he wrote:

> . . . there is a certain divine energy in every man, but sparing-
> ly employed as yet, which may be called the crank within—the
> crank after all—the prime mover in all machinery—quite indis-
> pensable to all work. Would that we might get our hands on its
> handle.[4]

I trust no reader will misconstrue this to be a plea on my part to
return to a vanished past of golden oak library furniture and hand-
written catalogue cards. This essay is being written on a word processor and I welcome its ease of correction, but I do not confuse the
convenience of what it offers with the value of the message. This is a
confusion we must be on guard against in our discussions on the role
of libraries in the research process. Let's foster convenience wherever we can but not enthrone it. Edwin Wolf reminds us:

> Candles, sputtering coal fires, quill pens, few books of refer-
> ence, and keepers of books whose main thrust was to keep out
> those who wanted to use them, and from this Johnson's *Dic-*

tionary, Adam Smith's *Wealth of Nations,* Gibbon's *Decline and Fall,* and hundreds of others.[5]

Librarianship today is out of balance in the relative emphasis given to the convergent and divergent aspects of the discipline. We have seen the symptoms growing over the last three decades in shifting attitudes toward reading, scholarship, and even faculty status for academic librarians. The notion that librarians may play a key role in fostering reading for pleasure, in encouraging the reading of what DeQuincey called the "literature of power" has given way to a narrower focus on the librarian as a processor of information. Our professional literature, though less humanistic and scholarly than we could wish, is still well ahead of the actual practice of librarianship in academic libraries.

Automation was to free librarians for less mechanical tasks and further the profession in its quest for intellectual parity with other disciplines in the academic community. And yet, paradoxically, the outlook for genuine faculty status darkened during the years when librarians became more proficient technicians. There are, indeed, some who seem to glory in the decline of the old librarianship. One recent writer exudes, "the genteel, scholarly, even dilettantish directors of the past are yielding to career-minded managers, administrators, and technicians."[6] One wonders if it is dilettantish to want librarianship to recapture the glory that was represented in some of those "directors of the past" such as Blanche McCrum, Louis R. Wilson, Lawrence Clark Powell, Guy Lyle, and John B. Nicholson, Jr., who exemplified the humanistic as well as the technological thrust of librarianship?

Here and there academic librarianship still offers us examples of those who seek to weave together the two strands of librarianship. Those who remember Neal Edgar (and who has forgotten him?) know how energetically he reflected both the humanistic and the technological strands. Whether it was a discussion on Edward Albee or James Agee, on the subtleties of *AACR* II or on the future of automation in librarianship, his views were eloquently expressed and closely reasoned. His standards were consistently high, and if you didn't meet those standards you might find your works consigned to one of his special manila folders labeled simply "Administration Atrocious," where he deposited the more sublimely idiotic memoranda and articles that passed his way. Yes, he is missed. We miss the laugh, we miss the generous help that he extended so freely, but perhaps most of all we miss the example of one for whom there was no conflict between the technical and the humanistic because in him the strands were woven so well as to be one.

Recently, I had the happy privilege of reading a brief private memoir of one of our country's most lively witted librarians. For over forty years this master teacher and librarian has contributed to the humanistic tradition of librarianship. What particularly interested me in his recollections of books, people, and libraries is the impact that several librarians had on his early life and their role in introducing him to the wonders of reading. These were librarians (women, incidentally) who felt that part of their task was to care and be present with the right books or at least the right words at the time when an eager young mind was first encountering the world of libraries. A magic chain began with these human encounters and this chain continues unbroken today in his own life and through the lives he has touched. One mentions such a story with a certain hesitation in this age of alleged sophistication. We have grown jaded with those who gush about the beauties of literature, about the importance of librarians liking books and people, about the role of books and libraries and teachers in the building of character. While such matters are often written of cloyingly, if we ignore them, we do so at our own peril, for they are at the heart of the humanistic tradition of librarianship.

Finally, if there is to be room in the libraries of tomorrow for the Friar Jeromes as well as the Brother Dominics, then libraries must offer some of the same rewards that John Updike says art offers:

> it offers . . . it seems to me . . . space—a certain breathing room for the spirit. The town I grew up in had many vacant lots; when I go back now, the vacant lots are gone. They were a luxury, just as tigers and rhinoceri, in the crowded world that is making, are luxuries. Museums and bookstores should feel, I think, like vacant lots—places where the demands on us are our own demands, where the spirit can find exercise in unsupervised play.[7]

The kind of libraries and librarians I have written about are also "luxuries" in an environment increasingly devoted to the efficient processing of information, and if they become extinct, the world of learning will be a poorer place.

REFERENCES

1. Schumacher, E.F., *A Guide for the Perplexed.* New York: Harper & Row, 1977. pp. 120-136.
2. Eliot, T.S., Choruses from "The Rock." *The Complete Poems and Plays.* New York: Harcourt, Brace & World, 1971. p. 96.
3. Schumacher, p. 123.
4. Thoreau, Henry David, *Miscellanies.* Boston: Houghton, Mifflin and Co., 1893. p. 59.
5. Wolf, Edwin, Library Dedication Speech, Cooperstown, N.Y., 1969.
6. Karr, Ronald Dale, "The Changing Profile of University Library Directors, 1966-1981," *College & Research Libraries,* (July 1984): p. 285.
7. Updike, John, " A Few Words in Defense of the Amateur Reader," *New York Times Book Review,* February 19, 1984, p. 7.

The Past Is Too Much With Us

John P. Comaromi

The past is too much with us. Mind you, I am not so modern-minded as to seek to greet each new day ignorant of what form its substance will take. I hope to greet it refreshed, not weary from a night's bout with yesterday's problems. When American librarians endeavor to provide the services for which they were hired and their libraries maintained (i.e., to acquire and organize information and the means to gain an education and to expedite the retrieval of both), upon their shoulders is a glacier's weight from the past.

Some practices from the past have their place in our present and future; they have proved their worth and should be continued. For instance, the call numbers for the books analyzed in *Essay and General Literature Index* should be inscribed next to the entries for them in the back of the *Index*; a more immediately helpful practice is difficult to find. However, some practices from the past frustrate our efforts to effect our ends.

General libraries are usually considered to belong to one of two sorts: research libraries and all the rest. That dichotomy is, of course, too crude. Let me suggest instead the model of a continuum along which each library falls according to the publics it serves. At one end is the archetype for the research library, at the other the archetype for the educational library. Every library falls somewhere on the continuum.

THE RESEARCH LIBRARY

The research library attempts to acquire, organize, and house documents that are or will be of value to its public. By "public" I mean all probable users of the library, not all possible users or beneficiaries of the library's materials. Possible users, of course, comprise a larger body than do actual users, and the beneficiaries of a library's use comprise the entire society, however large that is seen to be.

One using a research library normally seeks to retrieve items by way of their personal characteristics. The focus in on the item, and the item is sought through characteristics peculiar to it or to an extremely small class of works; that is, through the item's title, author, or series to which it belongs. It is reasonable to expect that each item be described in detail so that it can be distinguished from other items in the bibliographic universe. The normal user of the research library is the scholar whose mind is at the frontier that separates the known territory of their subject from *terra incognita*.

THE EDUCATIONAL LIBRARY

The educational library exists to mold the mind and to enable the mind to use information to produce the knowledge that will help to better the life of the seeker and society. That, of course, is the goal of the research library, at least in part; but there are several important differences between the two sorts of libraries. The first is that the users of an educational library are not scholars seeking to expand the frontiers of their field. By and large, only scholars use research libraries, while everyone, scholars included, use educational libraries. The next is that users of an educational library approach the items it contains through their subject matter; that is, they wish to learn about a certain subject, and are likely to learn about it through subject headings or the library's classification system. Thus what truly distinguishes the two kinds of libraries is how their users approach the materials in them: in the research library, the user is seeking a specific document; in the educational library the user is seeking those documents that represent the consensus of the educated upon a specific subject—that is, the best book on the subject (writings that are the most authoritative, understandable, recent, and available are the ones that should be found). A third marked difference between the two sorts of libraries is the rate of use of their materials: educational libraries expect heavy use of most documents; consequently, multiple copies of many items is the order of the day. Not so in research libraries; there multiple copies are forbidden, if not stamped out (remember the Bodleian discarding additional copies of the first folio of Shakespeare's works).

Educational libraries are those that we call public, school, junior college, and college libraries. Research libraries are those we call university and special libraries. The names are unfortunate, for they declare where the libraries are housed, not how they are used (except for special libraries, which are not included in this analysis).

The thought may already have crossed the reader's mind that a library can be both research and educational in the services it provides. Indeed it can, and that is why the model is a continuum upon which a library occupies a position according to the predominant type of service it provides—research or educational.

If a library misperceives its proper role and provides a research style of service rather than the educational one that its public is actually seeking, then it is disserving its public.

Though misperception of role causes problems, a more pernicious difficulty for the public that expect service from a library that falls at or near the midpoint of the continuum is that such a library cannot hope to perform two major roles successfully. It can serve either its research public well or its public seeking an education well. Though many libraries try to do so, they cannot serve both roles well simultaneously. The reasons for this are several: (1) Research libraries acquire a body of literature unfit for the needs of the educational library public primarily because the level of discourse is beyond that public's comprehension. (2) The public of educational libraries require thorough subject analysis of materials; the public of research libraries does not, and would probably resent it if provided. Indeed it may be impossible to assign precise subject headings to much of the material sought by the public of research libraries. (3) Research libraries' catalogs need detailed description and forms of entry that tend to confuse the public of educational libraries.

The research/educational continuum provides a useful model for explaining what has happened to American libraries during the past century, and what is likely to happen to them.

COLLECTIONS

It is in the nature of a research library to gather everything, in and out of sight, that may prove useful to its public. The extent of the material, however, is nothing short of light years long when laid cover to cover, and perceptive librarians have long ago concluded that they have neither the resources nor the space to acquire and house this material. Too few research libraries have come to this conclusion, unfortunately.

Research libraries generally continue to make readily available the bulk of their collections—at extraordinary expense. To be sure, their objective is to make available those items of value to their public. But what if 80% of their collections is never examined closely? What if 75% of their serials are never consulted? And of those serials that are consulted what if more than 80% of their use is of issues published within the five most recent years? This appears to be the case. Can anyone say that in the form of unused collections the past is not too much with research libraries?

To avoid the consuming past, research libraries need to make a horizontal division in their collections and in their catalogs. Only the past five year's production of monographs or serials should be readily accessible to their public. Older works should be stored in inexpensive lodgings. Those that have proved to have continuing use should be retained in the living collection. Likewise, the catalog should be divided horizontally; one would contain the records of the most recent five year collection, the other of the retired collection. (If the benefits of a single catalog are considered to be more desirable than this horizontal separation, then the location of the item can be gathered from its date of publication, which can be part of the call number or placed elsewhere on the record.)

Educational libraries suffer from the same malady as research libraries regarding retaining large parts of their collections that go unused, though expensively housed and obstructively present in the catalog in the form of clutter. Such a policy of retention is much more pernicious for educational libraries, for when patrons use outdated material from an educational library, they are unsuspectingly but decidedly misguided. Only unsuperseded works and belles-lettres should be retained among the current materials. All other deadwood prevents the library from fulfilling its designated role. Weeding and achieving maximum book availability are two processes that are too infrequently done in any sort of library. Weeding is essential not only to remove what is not used but more importantly to avoid misleading the public through offering obsolete information. And nothing defeats the educational library more than following policies that keep apart patrons and the works they seek: short hours, long loan terms, single copies, and no Cutter numbers almost guarantee that seekers will not turn to the educational library to find the information or work they are after. That weeding is done only fitfully and that book availability is rarely studied by librarians are sad facts.

The most misleading of pasts is the one that is no longer there. It is a measure of sanity and service that for each entry in a catalog there exists a work for which the entry stands. To ascertain that this is indeed the case libraries conduct inventories of their collections every five years or so—that is, many used to do so and a few still do. Entries for works no longer in the collection are removed from the catalog. As libraries grow, however, the periodic counting of owned items to rectify the catalog becomes onerous. And as works disappear from the collection (at an augmented rate during the late 1960s and 1970s), increasingly larger portions of catalogs are to phantom collections. During a study of the effect upon libraries of the phoenix (total) revisions of classes in the Dewey Decimal Classification, I saw an instance of the phenomenon of the phantom collection. One large public library that had long ago ceased doing inventory decided shortly after the publication of the eighteenth edition of the DDC—in which 510 Mathematics had received phoenix treatment—that the time was ripe to regain order in its mathematics collection. As the reclassification project progressed, the catalogers were stunned to discover that for every book retrieved for reclassification one could not be found. More than half of the cards in the catalog that directed the public to mathematical works were entries to a phantom mathematics collection. And surely the works gone were those most frequently sought. That is a past that denies us thought and the means to think.

CATALOGS

It is in the catalog and in the classification that educational libraries serve their publics least well. Not only, as we have seen above, is the past too much a part of our catalogs; it is the wrong past, the wrong present, and the wrong future. It is no secret that the major cataloging rules produced during the past three-quarters of a century—which all libraries use—were devised by and for research libraries. In fact, research libraries have captured the power to call for and to design the most important tool of our profession: cataloging rules.

CLASSIFICATION

In classification, as elsewhere, the needs of research libraries have affected the organization of educational libraries, Where item searching, rather than subject searching, is the focus of activity, there one finds acceptance of detailed description, entries by fullest form of the real name, and a classification that gives an address to an item. Whether the classification used collocates like materials—

that is to say, works upon the same or related subjects—is of secondary importance; what the classification has to do is give an address, and that quickly. Since it provides call numbers rather than class numbers only, the Library of Congress Classification does this better than the Dewey Decimal Classification (which has no centrally assigned author number or book number and suffers from being considered by many research libraries as not being quite up to snuff). Educational libraries, in my estimation better served by the DDC (but I am not without bias), have begun to switch to the LCC in the past few decades in the belief that what is good for research libraries must be good for them. Nothing could be further from the truth, and the disservice being done cannot be recompensed to the public of educational libraries. To be sure, the LCC does come with a complete address for an item. But those who made the decision to switch to the LCC seldom asked the public that uses its classification or the public services librarians who assist that public in its use whether either liked the neighborhoods into which the library's items were sent. It appears that public service librarians of research libraries who have worked with both classifications prefer the DDC. (That is on balance, of course; there are parts of the LCC that are considerably superior to the DDC.) It is not known what the public of educational libraries prefers in the way of a library classification. I am sure that what it wants is satisfactory results.

The simple fact is that the LCC was devised for a research library and in the eight decades of its existence no serious attempt has been made, nor is likely to be, to keep the system's structure current. Some educational libraries continue to switch to the LCC. When they learn that revision is no longer possible, they will come to understand that the past is with them permanently. They will also conclude that an up-to-date classification is of more value to them than the one they employ. I would like to say that the DDC will be that "up-to-date" classification, but that would be slightly dishonest. In several fields of study it will be decades before we can bring the DDC up to the structure that scholars of modern times admire.

CONCLUSION

What do I urge research librarians to do? Continue. What do I urge librarians of educational libraries to do? Why, face the future! Confront it! Do not believe for one minute that the public of educational libraries is best served by outdated collections and a shelf arrangement suited to closed collections. If you do believe that past structures are adequate for the future, then the past is too much with you. If you act upon your belief, the past will be too much with your public. And though it is in man's nature to cling to the past for solace, it is also in his nature to seek to survive—and that we can do only if the heavy hand of the past does not jeopardize our future.

The Sunny Book Review

Bill Katz

Librarians feel on occasion that it is absurd to read book reviews other than to find out about the inevitable plot, subject matter, or for whom intended. The reason is the almost total lack of negative opinion. Reviews are favorable, if not downright laudatory. This is hardly a tragedy, but by the same token it takes much of the zest out of life, and certainly does not help in collection development.

It is often remarked in studies and surveys of reviews that they express reverence for almost everything noticed. Comparing *Choice* and *Library Journal,* Macleod discovers what everyone has a sense of anyway—approximately 80 percent of all books reviewed are recommended.[1] Even a cursory glance through such diverse services as *Kirkus, The New York Times Sunday Book Review, Publishers Weekly, Time,* or just about any you care to consider, indicates much the same non-critical approach. About as close as any of these get to visible disappointment is the so-called "mixed" review, a euphemism for saying absolutely nothing.

The connection between criticism and simple notice of a new book is suggested by Neal Edgar's compilation of "Books and Book Reviews" for the fourth edition of *Magazines for Libraries.*[2] His close analytical annotations for 70 basic reviews reaffirms the conviction that few publish guilty verdicts.

Long ago *Booklist* did come to terms with the basic cause for good-natured reviews. Only recommended books are considered. If you see a title in *Booklist* it is approved for the library.

The rationale for avoiding the miserable, both by *Booklist* and others, is simple numbers. According to the *Bowker Annual* for 1983, "close to 50,000 books were published in 1982 in the United States." True, the total includes "approximately 4,500 mass market paperback titles and 12,000 more paperbacks," but this leaves a significant number of hardcover books for consideration—and, of course, does not rule out many of the paperbacks.[3] There is reason to think the number will increase for 1984 and through the 1980s.

Of those 50,000 books published, only 10 to 20 percent will be re-

17

viewed in the general media. *Choice* and *Booklist* notice from 6,500 to 7,000 each. Somewhat behind are *Library Journal* (about 5,000); *Kirkus* (near 4,500 to 5,000); and *Publishers Weekly* (some 5,000 to 5,500). Way, way back are the popular reviews—*Time* (about 300 titles) and the more ambitious *New York Times Sunday Book Review* with 2,500.[4]

In the infinite vastness of publishing output, the space taken by reviews is only a speck. Still, that speck does carry influence, if only to remind librarians and laypersons that X or Y title is available. The dilemma of the book review editor, for this is the individual who makes decisions about what is or is not considered, is to accomplish the impossible—select works likely to be of most interest to his or her readers.

The crucial step in the reviewing process is not the attitude of the reviewer. It is the decision of the editor to consider or not consider the book. The editor is by way of a benevolent censor. The built-in checks on the editor's disposition are competition and exposure. People will not continue to read a popular service where skepticism eliminates, for example, all fiction about short, brown dogs, or studies of eating habits and loss of weight. Animals and health fascinate too many, and when they are not pursued the reader will turn to other reviews. The ultimate concern of the book editor is to attract subscribers—an external which is often overlooked by critics struggling to understand the reviews.

Another factor checks the editor's responses. There is considerable repetition of books reviewed. If one service decides a swimming guide is of value, another is likely to reach the same conclusion. The overlap, for example, between *Choice* and *Library Journal* is obvious, although the former puts more emphasis on academic titles. At the same time, should the book editor not leap forward to review a book and it is subsequently noticed by two or three competitors, the book will be reconsidered for notice.

The editor has the ultimate control over both the number and what is reviewed but, coolly regarded, it is a power with definite limitations. Then, too, there is the sobering truth that reviewers don't always follow past patterns. The editor may mail out a book in the knowledge it is likely to be applauded, only to find that the otherwise congenial reviewer has had a bad breakfast and not only dislikes, but downright hates the title. This, let it be quickly added, does not happen often, or the editor and the reviewer are looking for new employment.

The one luxury the editor most emphatically does not have is the space to waste. Preferences must be for potentially valuable books. To deprive readers of information about a fair to good book on anthropology in favor of using the space to damn a treatise on physics serves no useful purpose. Since the numbers of what is published and the numbers of what is reviewed are totally out of balance, space must be expended on the good, not the bad, on the titles librarians should buy, not on those they should avoid. Well, at least that's the reasoning which accounts for the overwhelming number of favorable reviews.

There are two or three exceptions. The editor is not bound by an immutable law to rule out criticism, of telling what author or what works are disliked. Negative critical opinion particularly is necessary when the overcooked, tasteless prose is: (a) by a well-known author; (b) the object of publisher hype, i.e., a larger than average promotion budget; or (c) likely to be downright harmful and just as likely to be widely purchased because of the subject matter.

There are other reasons for seeking out potentially unfavorable reviews. The editor may disagree with the publisher's advertising policies. It has been rumored that failure to advertise in this or that journal may result not only in total neglect, but an occasional bad review. A less sinister reason for a cloudy notice is that the book review editor or the reviewer simply does not like the author, publisher or the jacket color. There are numerous entertaining and passionate explanations for the few bad reviews, some of which actually may have to do with the quality of the book.

In his essay, "Reading," W. H. Auden offers a justification for the good review, and one which any critic will completely appreciate. "Attacking bad books is not only a waste of time but also bad for the character. If I find a book really bad, the only interest I can derive from writing about it has to come from myself, from such display of intelligence, wit and malice as I can contrive. One cannot review a bad book without showing off."[5]

By this measure, few reviewers show off, and sometimes are polite to the point of absurdity. A case in point: the reviews of Norman Mailer's ride down the Nile, or Renata Adler's occasional thoughts disguised as a novel.

In a world where the majority of services faithfully visited by librarians are sunny and bright, how does one find a bit of welcome shade, or even a thunderstorm? In order to identify such a haven one must wish to be relieved from the self consciousness of good cheer and joy brought to the world by the reviewers. It is possible the majority don't want such relief. It is possible that some are uncomfortable with criticism, consider it as arbitrary as it is bad mannered. The evidence is meager, purely subjective and yet any effort to explain away the sunny reviews by other than numbers leaves one with the uncomfortable sense that there's more to it than book editors' choices. There is, perhaps, the notion held by readers that it is elitist to condemn.

Conversely, there is delight in sticking pins into pompous, wrong-headed writers and publishers. How many recall the scores of good reviews as contrasted with the single, devastating put down? The restless reader is amused and relieved by reviewers occasionally divorcing themselves from adjectives and adverbs of praise.

Emotional response, then, is mixed to criticism. A visual example of confusion is the film reviewer. On television he or she may ravage a new flick, much to the delight of the audience, only to be corrected by puzzled looks from the news staff. In a land where everything is right, what cause does the critic have to condemn? Committed to the good life, it is hard to imagine specific pain, particularly in criticism of anything.

Between masses of books being published every day, harassed editors with limited space, sometimes less-than-cooperative reviewers, and confusion as to the fairness of condemnation, it is hard to precisely explain the top-heavy good reviews.

What are the alternatives? Where can one find a less-than-sunny appreciation for everything published?

First, at least a small percentage of books are not recommended. In almost every issue of *Choice, Library Journal, The New York Times Sunday Book Review* and particularly *Kirkus* the voice of the crow is heard among the nightingales. There are always a few titles—less than 10 percent—which excite derision.

This author has a definite preference for the short notes in *Library Journal* and *Booklist* because they are much above average in descriptive strength and are fine signals to alert one to what is being published. At the same time, they are not necessarily satisfactory. There is no opportunity for the reviewer to be expansive, to paint a landscape instead of a line drawing of a central theme or topic. *The New York Review of Books* and *The Times Literary Supplement*, as well as *Nation, The New Yorker, The Village Voice*, and the *Saturday Review* allow movement for reviewers. At their finest the critics can be more fascinating than the books noticed.

Everyone has favored general reviews; but, essentially, what this means is favored reviewers. The second antidote to the music of optimism is to become acquainted with the reviewers themselves. For example, the most critical notes are to be found in the daily, not the Sunday, edition of *The New York Times.* Why? The answer is Christopher Lehmann-Haupt, and a number of other foes to purple prose. In *The New York Review of Books* almost anything by Gore Vidal, Stanley Hoffman or J. K. Galbraith is likely to be critical. *The New Yorker* is fine, but one can take exception to the building blocks of praise constucted by John Updike, or the overdone scholarship of George Steiner.

Despite—or is it because of—the vigorous selection of editors, a few individuals may be counted on to expose the bad, designate the best and the better. Again particular praise should go to the *Library Journal* where librarians warn one another of the more dangerous affronts to the sensibilities. One may be seduced, too, by the skill of the critics in *Choice,* but unfortunately, and for some baroque notion long ago dropped by *The Times Literary Supplement,* the names of the reviewers are not fixed to the annotations. The antiquated system defeats itself in that reviewers are dutifully noted in each number. It hardly takes an original mind to match a review of a work on the Chinese language with the one reviewer teaching Chinese.

The importance of the caustic, identified reviewer is summarized by Auden: "If, when a reviewer whose taste I trust condemns a book, I feel a certain relief, this is only because so many books are published that it is a relief to think—'Well, here at least, is one I do not have to bother about.' "[6]

For example, in reviews of literature there is some respite, although the cold critical voice is distant. When it does sound, it is like a blast. Again, as with individual reviewers, one must come to appreciate the individual literary journals. Still, from the *Antioch Review* to *Southern Review,* the same problems plague the editors. There is never enough space. As a result the average journal reviews no more than 50 to 60 titles a year. Comparatively, in 1982 some 1,450 literature titles were published. The other difficulty of particular interest to librarians is that it takes about seven months from receipt of the completed book review to publication.

Unlike the general library review media, the journals have the advantage of longer reviews (usually 750 to 1500 words, as compared with 100 to 200 words, say, in *Library Journal*) which in turn allows more consideration of the faults. [This is true, of course, of *The Times Literary Supplement* and *The New York Review of Books*, and to a lesser extent, the daily and Sunday *New York Times* and the *Washington Post Book World.*] Even here, though, they are never long enough for the critics who argue "that removal of restraints on length may produce more astute analysis."[7]

The same configurations of difficulty are to be found in other subject, scholarly and specialized journals, which explains why they are not an elaborate, important source of guidance for librarians, although they may be for individuals. As a defensive wall against the good humor man, they do serve a purpose. Within their limited, late enclosure they often note books not found earlier, or at any time in the general reviews.

Librarians do have a distinct advantage in that there are several reviewing media which parallel the professional interests. The reference librarian, for example, may turn to *RQ, Reference Services Review, American Reference Books Annual,* and, of course, the *Reference Books Bulletin* (formerly: *Reference and Subscription Books Review*)—to name the outstanding services dedicated to the reference shelf. It is well-nigh impossible to find complete sunshine in any of these. They can't help but arouse enthusiasm for good old hard-hitting criticism.[8]

There are instances when even they falter, and once again the reader becomes more involved with the individual critic than with the medium itself. It's too bad the *Reference Books Bulletin* refuses to give due credit to the wisdom and grandeur of the individual, continues to hide behind a committee. One may applaud the prodigality of the committee and its editor, yet long to make the acquaintance of the librarian who has the temerity to end a review with the simple declaration: "not recommended." Let the reviewers rise up and demand well-deserved attention.

Actually, it really seems to make little or no difference which stand is taken. "The data indicates that for books with one, two, five or six reviews there may be no significant relationship between the direction of the reviews a book receives and the inclusion of that book in libraries."[9] This shatters the nostalgic notion which governs book review critics. Perhaps they simply don't matter. The only thing that really matters is that the book be noticed—good, bad, or indifferent.

One dubious method of charting the storm in the sunshine is to learn to read between the lines, to be able to translate "bookspeak." Manifestations of this peculiar language are found in certain key words and phrases such as sophisticated (read: too much sex); gentle (nothing happens); articulate (about the Tarzan and Jane level); movie material (lots of gore, mayhem, and violence) and so on.[10] The injunction is to take nothing literally in a review.

Before moving on to a suggested solution for the lack of critical reviews, it is only fair to consider a darker side to the whole business. One may long for credible scorn, yet realize it brings sorrow. When mild to harsh evaluations do surface they are not always justified and sometimes they can be a painful experience to the writer.[11] Professional authors develop necessary antibodies, but for the less-than-experienced, the embarassing review can be a nightmare. Catharsis usually is effected by another critic, who inevitably is more charitable and, if in the mainstream of the media, will be downright favorably inclined. Still, the wronged author longs for revenge. One suspects that the sometimes really wicked judgments evolve when the author's turn comes to pen a review of his reviewer's efforts.

What is worse than a bad review, is no review. Even with thousands of specialized journals the majority of the 50,000 books published each year are not even noticed. The silent effect particularly is obvious to first-time authors.

In *Writer's Choice: A Library of Rediscoveries* there are listed and annotated over 1,000 books selected by some 400 well known writers.[12] They have one thing in common—most are undeservedly overlooked, neglected or otherwise forgotten. It's a pity because all are not only worth attention, but are equal or far superior to the majority of books dutifully and favorably reviewed each year. While some of them did receive attention when published, most did not, or, at best, were reviewed without feeling or appreciation.

Why this failure to not only not take notice, but to register neither a yea or nay vote? Let one disappointed photographer explain:

> It's possible that the general neglect of the small press by the major media has no real reason, no real policy, no real thought. It could quite easily be arbitrary, contingent, completely indeterminate. We are probably not paranoid, but simply naive about the operation of large institutions if we imagine the book editor . . . [has] planned to neglect our efforts.[13]

Books can be promoted in other ways and studies seem to indicate that librarians (and individuals) are inclined to purchase a book which is advertised. A direct mail promotion may not be better than a review, but it will overcome lack of attention and even the occasional nasty judgment.[14] Again, though, the problem is where is the money for these advertisements and promotions? The contentious librarian may say at this point—so what? The reviews are favorable, they do not cover even the majority of books published, but they are better than nothing, certainly better than advertisements, and they help. True, yet would it not be helpful to have, say, double the number of reviews?

The answer, which is arbitrary and hardly original, is simplicity itself. Many journals publish totally useless lists of "books received" which may or may not (and usually it is the latter) be reviewed. Why not go one step further? After each title put a plus or a minus, or a recommended or not recommended, or provisionally recommended. That's all. This could be done by the experienced editor. At the same time the librarian is given due warning about what is really bad, is afforded the opportunity to order (if only on approval) books which are recommended, yet are not thoroughly reviewed.

Particular stress should be placed on the not-recommended signal. If this is done conscientiously, and with sensibility, the librarian will be saved thousands of dollars in less-than-necessary purchases—one suspects as much from jobbers and approval plans as anything else.

This service could be appended to all of the major library book review media—from *Kirkus* and *Library Journal* to *Choice* and *Booklist*. It would be fascinating, after all, to see what titles *Booklist* simply overlooks, or does not think worthy of review.

Book reviews today, as Neal so well knew and so carefully explained, are an expression of sometimes harmless good will, doomed to give only a glimpse of what is published. If, for whatever cause, this is the situation, there is equally no reason it can't be reversed. Is it either innocent or frivolous to ask for a change, to ask, indeed, for a little gloom in the land of book review sunshine?

REFERENCES

    1. Macleod, Beth, "Library Journal and Choice: A Review of Reviews," *The Journal of Academic Librarianship,* (March, 1981): 23-28.
    2. Katz, Bill (ed.). *Magazines for Libraries.* New York: R. R. Bowker, 1982. pp. 173-187.

3. "Book Trade Research and Statistics." In *The Bowker Annual of Library & Book Trade Information,* 28th ed. New York: R. R. Bowker, 1983, p. 371.

4. *Ibid,* p. 405. For an overview of the number of books reviewed by popular magazines, as well as policies, see: Gorman, Trisha, "Which Books Should Get Review? How Ten Magazines Choose," *Publishers' Weekly,* 220 (November 6, 1981): 23-26.

5. Auden, W. H. *The Dyer's Hand.* New York: Random House, 1962, p. 11.

6. *Ibid.*

7. Budd, John, "Book Reviewing Practices of Journals in the Humanities," *Scholarly Publishing,* 13 (July, 1982): 370.

8. For a summary of current reference review practices see Bunge, Charles, "Reviewing of Adult Reference Materials for General Libraries," *The Reference Librarian,* (Fall/Winter, 1981): 21-29.

9. Serebnick, Judith, "Book Reviews and the Selection of Potentially Controversial Books in Public Libraries," *Library Quarterly,* 51 (No. 4, 1981): 400. At the same time, the author found that "for books with three or four reviews, a significant relationship is likely to exist." (p. 400). The point of the rather ambiguous finding is to underline what publishers, reviewers and librarians know: the important thing is for the book to be reviewed, good, bad or indifferent. The review usually is enough to spark a sale.

10. "Book Reviewing Vocabulary," *The Unabashed Librarian,* (No. 40, 1981): 12.

11. Stern, Madeline, "Reviewers Reviewed: The Author's Perspective," *AB Bookman's Weekly,* 68 (November 9, 1981): 3183-3190.

12. Katz, Linda Sternberg and Bill Katz, *Writer's Choice: A Library of Rediscoveries.* Reston, VA: Reston/Prentice Hall, 1983.

13. Perkins, David, "The Beast and the Burden: The Major Press and its Coverage of Small Press Publications," *Show-Me Libraries,* 34 (October/November, 1982): 33.

14. Smith, Malcolm, "Books Selection Sources," *Library Association Record,* 81 (March, 1979): 131.

Financing the Public Libraries of Ohio: A Problem in Resource Allocation

A. Robert Rogers

For over half a century the State of Ohio has had a unique method of funding public libraries. Unlike most other states[1] (and indeed most other countries in the English-speaking world), Ohio does not depend primarily on local property taxes to support its public libraries. The historical background has been summarized by Walter Brahm:

> Until 1921, most public libraries in Ohio were either the association or municipal type with a few organized as school district, township, county and county district. Prior to that time, the legislature passed a 15-mill limitation on real property taxes and sub-divisions which had been levying up to a mill and a half tax for libraries suddenly found themselves unable to do so. However the right of school districts to levy outside this limitation was re-established in 1921. Since school districts thus were exempt from this limitation any library which might be organized as a part of a school district could levy a tax of one and a half mills. This caused many of the association and municipal libraries to change their form of organization whereby they re-organized under the school district. However, in 1929, effective in 1931, the people of Ohio voted a constitutional limitation of 15 mills—reduced to 10 mills in 1934—on all real property, making this apply also to school districts. When this happened school district libraries and all other public libraries which had been supported by real property taxes were entirely without support. Theoretically they were—and still are—entitled to support from property tax if they could get it, but in actual practice it amounted to cutting off the libraries' source of income because other sub-divisions would have had to share the funds they received within the 15 mills. . . .[2]

Legislation, sponsored by Robert A. Taft, then State Senator from Hamilton County, and enacted by the Ohio General Assembly in 1931 provided a new funding base for the public libraries of Ohio—the local situs intangible tax, collected at the county level, primarily from individuals on income from stocks, bonds and other productive investments. (Technically, it is a classified property tax which also includes unproductive investments and the property of corporations operating in only one county.)[3] Since 1933, the intent of the law has been clarified and its implementation refined as a consequence of a series of court cases and legislative amendments.[4]

In 1983, the Administration proposed, and the General Assembly enacted, as part of the budget bill (Am. Sub. H. B. 291), the repeal of local situs intangible tax, effective January 1, 1986,[5] and its replacement by a Library and Local Government Support Fund, consisting of 6.3% of the revenue from the state income tax.[6] The new legislation provided that the state would send to each county an amount equal to its proportionate share of the statewide total of the proceeds from the local situs intangible tax in 1985.[7] Each county, in turn, was to distribute this money to public libraries and other units of local government in amounts equal to their proportionate shares of the 1985 distribution of proceeds from the local situs intangible tax.[8] The legislation also stated:

There is hereby created a Public Library Financing and Support Committee consisting of twelve members including two members of the House of Representatives who are members of the House Finance-Appropriations Committee and two members of the Senate who are members of the Senate Finance Committee. One member of the House of Representatives and one member of the Senate shall be members of the majority party appointed by the Speaker of the House of Representatives and President of the Senate, respectively, and one member of the House of Representatives and one member of the Senate shall be members of the minority party appointed by the Minority Leader of the House of Representatives and Minority Leader of the Senate, respectively. The other eight members shall be appointed by the Governor and shall consist of one representative of the investment banking industry, five representatives of the library community, and two consumers. The library representatives shall be selected from a list of at least ten persons submitted to the Governor by the Ohio Li-

brary Association and the Ohio Library Trustees Association.
The Governor shall designate one of the members of the committee to serve as Chairman. All appointments shall be made
within 30 days of the effective date of this section. Vacancies
on the committee shall be filled in the same manner as the original appointments. The committee shall study the existing
method of funding public libraries, procedures for the distribution of funding, and the adequacy of funding levels throughout
the state. The committee may request staff assistance from the
Tax Commissioner, the State Library, and the Legislative Service Commission. Not later than January 1, 1985, the committee shall submit a report to the Governor and to the General
Assembly setting forth the committee's recommendations pertaining to the public support of public libraries, together with
suggested legislation to complement the committee's recommendations.

The method of funding prescribed by sections 5707.051,
5747.03, and 5747.49 of the Revised Code shall remain in effect until changed by law.[9]

The major issue to be addressed by the Public Library Financing
and Support Committee is whether the distribution methods and
ratios specified in the 1983 legislation are appropriate for the indefi-
nite future or whether alternative approaches should be recommended to the Governor and the General Assembly. The comments
that follow, though written by a member of the Committee, are personal opinions intended to make a contribution to the clarification
and discussion of issues. They are in no sense a statement on behalf
of the Committee, though it is hoped that they may be useful to the
Committee in its deliberations.

The issue of distribution is one of long standing in Ohio and one
on which little direct guidance is available from the public library
experience of other states, because the typical public library is supported by local property taxes levied by the taxing authority of the
jurisdiction which it serves and thus is not directly in competition
with other public libraries for funds from a common tax source.[10]
Considerable indirect guidance is available, however, if the problem is stated more broadly as one of resource allocation. Whether
the resource to be allocated is time, personnel or money, needs must
be identified and priorities determined. The Mayor of New York,
for example, must weigh the competing demands of the uniformed

services, the public schools, the city hospitals, and the public library. The director of a large public library must allocate resources
(personnel, materials, funding) to the central library and the branches in relation to such factors as populations of the neighborhoods
served and volume of library activities (e.g., circulation, reference,
program attendance). Criteria for allocation of state aid to public libraries provide further clues as do criteria used by state boards of
higher education to allocate funds to colleges and universities. Additional insight can be gained from studies by the Centre for Interfirm
Comparison for the British Library and by the work of the Public
Library Association which culminated in *Output Measures for Public Libraries* (Chicago: American Library Association, 1982).
Finally, there is experience in Ohio from more than fifty years of allocation by county budget commissions in those counties where several public libraries compete with one another and with other units
of local government for intangible tax funds.

In summarizing information from *State Aid: A Survey Report*
(Chicago: Association of Specialized and Cooperative Library
Agencies, 1982), Despres and Vincent noted that:

> Per capita aid distributed in proportion to population served
> was the frequently cited formula for grants to local libraries.
> This method of distribution was used by 78% of the states
> making direct grants to local libraries. Second was the basic
> grants-in-aid method, which was used by 44% of the states
> making direct grants to local libraries. This method is charac-
> terized by equal dollar grants to libraries, sometimes varied by
> size or class of library. Of less popularity are discretionary
> grants (41%). Equalization grants and partial reimbursement
> of local expenditures (defined as payments of a specified por-
> tion of local expenditure for specified purposes, such as eligi-
> ble capital project costs) were used less frequently by the states
> (31% and 28% respectively). Only 16% of the states making
> direct grants to local libraries base their distribution in whole
> or part upon area (square mileage) grants.[11]

The literature on state funding for higher education is voluminous
and only a few key examples can be cited here. Caruthers and Orwis
described five approaches: incremental budgeting, formula budgeting, program budgeting, zero-based budgeting, and performance
budgeting. A key problem which they identified was that of equity,

allocating similar resources for similar needs.[12] Gross found a substantial increase in the use of formula budgeting since its introduction in 1951.[13] In a 1976 study for the Michigan State Department of Education, it was found that 25 of the 50 states used formulas in allocating funds for higher education.[14] Most formulas emphasize the number of full-time equivalent (FTE) students, with subsidies weighted according to discipline (more for the natural sciences which require expensive laboratory equipment, less for the humanities and social sciences) and program level (doctoral, master's, upper division and lower division, in descending order). Enrollment-driven formulas proved more satisfactory in times of expansion than in times of steady state or decline. Many formulas now differentiate between fixed costs (e.g., maintenance, utilities) and variable costs (e.g., instruction, student services). In recent years, the Ohio Board of Regents has modified its formulas. The formula for instruction for 1983/84 has 16 levels, ranging from $789 at General Studies I to $11,261 at Medical II. Library acquisitions and plant operations (to take but two examples) now have separate formulas which are not enrollment driven.[15]

The Centre for Interfirm Comparison "was established as an independent non-profit organization in 1959 by the British Institute of Management and the British Productivity Council specifically to meet the demand for a neutral, expert body to conduct interfirm comparisons as a service to management."[16] In recent years, the Centre has conducted studies on non-profit organizations in addition to its surveys of businesses. Following a feasibility study for the British Library in 1977, the Centre undertook a pilot project and received data from 27 public libraries of various sizes. The analysis of resource allocation in relation to work done focused on "the *use of libraries' resources* and on the *services provided to users.*"[17] The study included operating costs (staff, premises, library materials, other) and capital costs.[18] Other factors studied included:

> The population density, age and employment structure and the proportion of children remaining at school after school leaving age . . . . Low densities may call for much provision through mobile or part-time libraries at different costs per issue from those of large service points; more retired people, professional workers and those staying at school longer may make above-average demands on library services.

Two ratios are used to give general indicative measures of

the use of made by people of their library systems. These are
the number of registered readers and issues per 1,000 population. . . . Registered readership figures are thought by some
to be a more reliable reflection of numbers of current library
users if readers have to re-register frequently. . . . [19]

Staff costs ranged from a low of 43% to a high of 59%. The medians
for the four categories (county libraries, Scottish districts, London
boroughs, metropolitan boroughs) ranged from a low of 48% to a
high of 57%. (The arithmetic mean of the four medians was
53.5%.) Premises costs ranged from a low of 9% to a high of 26%.
The medians for the four categories ranged from a low of 12% to a
high of 16%. (The arithmetic mean of the four medians was
14.25%.) Library materials costs ranged from a low of 17% to a
high of 29%. The medians ranged from a low of 21% to a high of
24%. The arithmetic mean of the four medians was 23%. The cost
of other operations ranged from a low of 5% to a high of 15%. The
medians ranged from a low of 9% to a high of 13%. The arithmetic
means of the medians was 10.75%.[20] Although the arithmetic means
of the medians add up to 101.5%, the composite picture is sugges-
tive: staff—53.5%; premises—14.25%; library materials— 23%;
other—10.75%. The number of registered readers per 1,000 population in 1978/79 ranged from a low of 412 to a high of 708.9. (To
use American parlance, the number of registered borrowers in relation to the populations of the primary service areas ranged from
41.2% to 70.78%.) The medians ranged from a low of 441.9 to a
high of 569.3. The arithmetic mean of the four medians was 487.2.[21]
(If the sample is representative, nearly half of the people in Britain
make some use of their public libraries.) The number of issues (cir-
culations) per 1,000 population in 1978/79 ranged from a low of 9.2
to a high of 14.7. The medians ranged from a low of 11.1 to a high
of 13.5. The arithmetic mean of the four medians was 11.95.[22] The
number of library staff per 100,000 population served ranged from
a low of 29.3 to a high of 63.4. The medians ranged from a low of
40.1 to a high of 60.1. The arithmetic mean of the four medians was
48.55.[23] The differences between the United Kingdom and the
United States and the differences in goals and objectives among
public library systems would suggest caution in the interpretation
and use of these data. Nevertheless, they do provide some useful
clues concerning factors to be considered in developing a fund
allocation formula or process.

The first standards for public libraries were issued by the American Library Association in 1934. Substantial changes occurred during the postwar years, culminating in *Standards for Public Library Systems* (Chicago: American Library Association, 1966).[24] The emphasis on large systems in the 1966 standards left a gap with respect to small and medium-sized libraries and many states (including Ohio) developed standards of their own to compensate. The most recent version is *Standards for the Public Libraries of Ohio* (Columbus: Ohio Library Association, 1980). These standards cover accessibility, structure and government, program, materials, personnel, and physical facilities. They contain useful clues for the development of an allocation formula in that acceptable ranges of expenditure ratios are provided for the following broad categories: materials (books, periodicals, audiovisual, other)—15-25%; personnel (salaries and fringe benefits)—50-70%; operations (supplies, building repairs, rental contracts, utilities, etc.)—15-25%.[25] The cost of implementing these standards was studied by the Ohio Library Association during 1982/83 and was found to be $17.99 per capita in 1981 dollars.[26]

Standards for public libraries have not been issued at the national level in nearly 20 years. The principal reason is that thinking about standards has undergone a veritable revolution in the intervening period. Traditional standards tended to concentrate on *inputs* (facilities, budget, staff, collection) and to assume that a proper level of inputs would result in a desirable level of *outputs* (services to library users). In the 1970s, attention was turned to what a public library actually delivers to its community in return for the tax dollars spent. The appearance of *Performance Measures for Public Libraries* in 1973 both marked a radical departure from the traditional thinking and served as a stimulus for further research. This pioneering study attempted to develop measurements for the following basic services:

1. Making materials available to users
2. Providing facilities to users
3. Making staff available to users.[27]

The change in direction away from national standards based on inputs accelerated in the late 1970s. Emphasis began to be placed on goal setting to meet local community needs and on a planning process which might be used by local libraries to develop and carry out their objectives. These efforts culminated in *A Planning Process for Public Libraries,* by Vernon E. Palmer and others (Chicago: American Library Association, 1980). The apparent abandonment of the effort to develop standards at the national level led the Oklahoma Department of Libraries and the Oklahoma Library Association to enter into a contract with King Research, Inc., of Rockville, Maryland, to produce studies that would be of assistance to statewide planners and those responsible for local public libraries in Oklahoma.[28] Four types of measures were adopted:

1. *Community penetration* (circulation per capita; community awareness of library services; users as a percentage of population; registered borrowers as a percentage of population);
2. *User services* (title fill rate; subject fill rate; reference questions per capita; adult program attendance per adult capita; juvenile program attendance per juvenile capita; juvenile percentage of circulation/juvenile percentage of materials budget; juvenile percentage of circulation/juvenile percentage of population; interlibrary loan fill rate; information and referral services checklist);
3. *Resource management* (collection turnover rate; range of hours open; ratio of staff to population; ratio of staff to circulation; square footage per capita; items held per capita; percentage of holdings intended for juveniles; cooperative activities checklist; collection checklist);
4. *Administration and finance* (per capita support; local library funds as percentage of total local budget; materials as percent of total expenditures; salaries and wages as percent of total expenditures; percentage of staff participating in continuing education; administrative checklist).[29]

The Illinois Library Association opted for a middle ground between the traditional approach and the newer emphasis on output measures in its 1982 standards which covered the following topics: structure and governance; finances; administration; community and interagency cooperation; public relations; accessibility; users and usage; services (reference, specific populations, programs); personnel; materials; physical facilities; system and ILLINET membership responsibilities.[30] The research in Oklahoma and Illinois was crossfertilized by studies at the national level undertaken by the Goals, Guidelines and Standards Committee of the Public Library Association which resulted in the issuance of a manual for gathering data on the following output measures: circulation per capita; in-library materials use per capita; library visits per capita; program attendance per capita; reference transactions per capita; reference fill rate; title fill rate; subject and author fill rate; browsers' fill rate; registration as a percentage of population; turnover rate, and document delivery.[31]

None of the studies cited in the preceding paragraphs contains a ready-made solution to the distribution problem affecting the public libraries of Ohio, but useful clues that may be pieced together can be gleaned from them. Further clues may be gleaned from a review of attempts in Ohio to grapple with the distribution question.

The first issue relating to distribution was the priority of libraries in relation to other units of local government. Before 1951, the law provided that the proceeds of the local situs intangible tax should be distributed "according to the relative needs of the libraries and other units entitled to share in the distribution of such taxes." The claim that libraries should have first consideration was strengthened by legislation enacted by the General Assembly in 1951 to the effect that distribution should be made to libraries "based on the needs of such libraries." The 1953 decision by the Ohio Supreme Court in the case of Montgomery County Library Trustees vs Montgomery County Budget Commission was particularly critical in affirming library priority up to the level of "needs."[32]

As the proportion of the proceeds from the local situs intangible tax distributed to libraries began to reach 100% in more and more counties, a new issue came to the fore: criteria for weighing the relative needs of competing library systems within a county. This issue was partially addressed by the State Library Board in a statement adopted on April 7, 1970 entitled "Factors in the Allocation of Intangibles Tax Funds." The ten factors identified were: historical background; costs of maintaining present facilities and services; population of primary service area; distribution and relationship to number of users; extension possibilities; nature of library's collection; special services to the handicapped and disadvantaged; existing unmet needs; balance between need for operating and capital funds; cooperative planning; good administrative practice.[33] Beginning in 1973, representatives of the seven library systems in Summit County began to work on a formula that would take many of these factors into account. In 1974, a formula was adopted which used 1974 as a base year and began a gradual phasein process in 1975. The phasein was very gradual because the formula was applied only to funds in excess of those received in the base year. By 1979, the formula was being applied to 28% of the available funds. There were four components (equally weighted and with tables of calculations provided) in the Summit County formula: *Units of service* (interpreted as circulation of books, recordings and films); *Population served* (annual estimates for the current and two preceding years); *Physical plants* (with two subcomponents—number of physical plant units and total square footage); *Survey formula* (an adjustment to take income disparity into account).[34] Further study of formula distribution was done by a committee of the Ohio Library Trustees Association which presented a report to the OLTA Board of Directors on May 6, 1981. After noting the importance of a county-wide trustee agreement and the relevance of *Handbook for Ohio Library Trustees* (Columbus: Ohio Library Trustees Association, 1978), the committee identified four elements to be included in a formula: *The public served* (population of the primary service area); *Use of the library collection* (circulation); *The physical plant* (with two subcomponents, number of physical plants and total square footage); and *Potential library utilization* (inverse weighting by income brackets of the number of families in each library's primary service area). All of the four elements were equally weighted. Tables showing the calculations were provided.[35] These earlier studies were utilized in 1983 by Touche Ross & Company in the development of a recommended formula for distribution of the proceeds of the local situs intangible tax to the nine public libraries of Cuyahoga County. The recommendations were "tailor-made" to the situation in Cuyahoga County and included a substantial "set aside" (approximately 17%) to be taken "off the top" and allocated to the Cleveland Public Library in recognition of the unique role of the CPL Main Library in providing reference/research services for the entire metropolitan area. The remainder of the funds were to be allocated by formula. *Output Measures for Public Libraries* (Chicago: American Library Association, 1982) was examined for factors that might be included in a formula. In general, it was found that per capita measures, while immensely valuable for internal management, are not helpful in a tax allocation formula where total volume of activity (e.g., circulation) is needed for each library in order to determine its proportionate share of the county total. Several promising factors (e.g., library visits) had to be eliminated because the libraries do not presently maintain such records. Although it was recognized that determination of relative weights was more a matter of informed opinion than an exact science, some weighting was attempted. The factors in the proposed formula and the recommended weights are as follows:

1. *Population and service area*—40% (population—30%; income disparity—5%; size of service area—5%);
2. *Library use*—40% (circulation—30%; reference transactions—5%; program attendance—5%);
3. *Facilities and resources*—20% (number of plants—5%; usable library space—5%; hours open per week—5%; collections—5%.[36]

An acceptable distribution formula will probably require further refinement of the elements noted in the preceding paragraphs, with particular attention to the matter of weighting. Before addressing that issue, it may be well to look at the distribution question from a statewide perspective and to review attempts to solve that problem in recent years.

From a statewide perspective, the distribution problem is extremely serious. Any tax levied and collected at the local or county level is likely to exhibit disparities between wealthy and poor areas. With the local situs intangible tax, these disparities have been extreme. In 1982, for example, only $36,743 was collected in Monroe County, contrasted with $29,012,818 in Cuyahoga County. On a per capita basis, collections ranged from $1.69 in Lawrence County to $26.59 in Hamilton County. Per capita distributions to libraries ranged from $1.69 in Lawrence County to $20.83 in Geauga County.[37] The situation in 1982 appeared to be little different from that in 1977:

> 79% of the books, 84% of the library staff, and 82% of the tax income are in the libraries of only 13 counties. While $7.86 was the average per capita public library expenditure in 1977, only 8 counties reached or passed that level. 57% of all funds expended for public library services in 1977 was expended in those 8 counties. In the same year the per capita income of libraries was 11 times as much in the highest county ($12.51) as in the lowest ($1.14).[38]

In the 1930s, Ohio developed a program of state aid, administered by the State Library, to address some of these problems. With the advent of substantial federal funding under the Library Services and Construction Act (LSCA) of 1964, the State Library of Ohio commissioned a series of studies by Ralph Blasingame, of Rutgers University, to address the issue of library development. A key recommendation was that regional library systems be developed, using a combination of federal and state funds to provide "organizational or establishment grants and continuing support grants." A formula for funding was also developed.[39] During the spring and summer of 1968, Blasingame's recommendations were studied and modified by representatives of the Ohio Library Association and the Ohio Library Trustees Association. The resulting Ohio Library Development Plan, which was unanimously adopted by both organizations at their annual conferences in October 1968, recommended the creation of Area Library Service Organizations (ALSOs) in which local libraries in groups of continuous counties would cooperate without losing local identity. A combination of federal and state funding was to be used to provide:

1. Planning grants to assist libraries within an area to prepare plans for use of essential services operation grants. . . .
2. Establishment grants, during the formative stage for equipment, bookstock, etc., but not buildings.
3. Essential services operation grants to be distributed between the several counties on a formula which will be basically the difference between the average statewide per capita operating income of public libraries in the state from tax sources, less the average countywide per capita operating income available to the public libraries in a county from such taxes.[40]

These and other provisions relating to Area Library Service Organizations were enacted into law in 1969.[41] Funding was sought, unsuccessfully, from the General Assembly in 1971. In 1973, funds appropriated to the State Library for the state aid program which began in the 1930s were consolidated and used (along with some federal funds) to begin the first ALSO (Ohio Valley Area Libraries, OVAL) as a pilot project. It was hoped that the success of this project would encourage the General Assembly to provide full state funding for OVAL and state funding for other ALSOs. Meanwhile, most of the state was blanketed with multicounty library cooperatives, using a combination of federal (LSCA) and local funding. State funding for ALSOs was sought every biennium from 1971 to 1979 but was not forthcoming from the General Assembly.

In the late 1970s and early 1980s the Ohio Library Association and the Ohio Library Trustees Association studied alternative approaches to alleviate the worst effects of income disparity among the public libraries of Ohio. One approach was to take *Standards for the Public Libraries of Ohio,* develop per capita cost figures for implementing those standards, and calculate the total cost if all public libraries were supported at that level. Assuming continuation of the local situs intangible tax, local levies and other sources of local library income, the state's share would be the difference between local revenues and what was needed to bring all libraries up to OLA standards. This proposed program was described as "supplemental state support." As a result of studies conducted during 1982/83, it was estimated that the annual cost for the 1984/85 biennium (in 1981 dollars) would have been $68,787,205.[42]

An alternative approach (similar to the funding concepts of the Ohio Library Development Plan described above) would be to take the statewide average per capita income from the local situs intangible tax for the preceding year (or biennium) and calculate the cost of bringing counties below the statewide average up to the statewide average. In 1982, the statewide average was $12.29 per capita. Only 10 counties met or exceeded that average. To have brought the other 78 counties up to the 1982 statewide average would have required $26,725,109.[43]

With this background, it is time to return to the question of a distribution formula. Such a formula should meet the following criteria:

1. *Comprehensiveness.* It should include all factors that have a significant bearing on library costs;
2. *Equity.* It should reward similar activities in a similar fashion;
3. *Balance.* It should preserve excellence where it already exists and support improvements in underserved areas;
4. *Simplicity.* It should be sufficiently straightforward that staffs in libraries of all sizes are able to understand and apply it.

There appear to be three distinct categories of measures that should be considered for possible inclusion: service obligation; library provision; and community response. All three appear to be of approximately equal importance.

Measures of *service obligation* must include population of the primary service area, whether a school district, a municipality, or some other unit. Although county budget commissions are not required to make explicit the reasons for their decisions, a cursory examination of library allocations would suggest that population is a major factor. This is an eminently reasonable approach. It does depend, however, on reasonably precise understandings within each county of the primary service areas of the different public libraries—something that is not always easy to do, especially in rural counties where consolidations of school districts have rendered library boundaries unclear. Libraries which serve disadvantaged neighborhoods must usually exert greater effort for more limited returns than libraries in more affluent communities. The inclusion of this factor is controversial—and the weight to be assigned even more so. But it cannot be entirely ignored. Finally, the size of a library's service area needs to be considered. The cost of operating and maintaining vans to deliver to widely-scattered branches or bookmobiles to serve remote areas has risen sharply in recent years. The universality of population as a factor in the formulas already examined suggests that it should be assigned a heavy weight. The relative infrequency of occurrence of the other two factors would suggest lesser weights. The following seem reasonable: population—25; income disparity—5; size of service area—5.

Measures of *library provision* are largely the traditional measures of input. The number of facilities must be considered. This is a measure of access. The number of square feet of usable library space should also be included. This is a measure of public comfort and convenience. The number of hours open per week is another measure of access. The size of the staff is a measure of the help available to users of the library. The size of the acquisitions budget is a measure of commitment to providing that most basic commodity which a library offers its public—books and other library materials for home reading/viewing/listening or for consultation within the library. Some indication of appropriate relative weighting may be gleaned from the work of the Centre for Interfirm Comparison and *Standards for the Public Libraries of Ohio.* "Premises" accounted for close to 15% of library expenditures when the CIFC figures were averaged out. Staff accounted for between 50% and 55%. Library materials accounted for about 23%. These are also within the acceptable ranges in the OLA standards. Using a total weight of 35 for this category, the following divisions thus appear reasonable: number of facilities—3; square feet of usable space—2; hours open per week—3; size of staff—18; size of collection—9.

The final stage in the process is to measure the *community re-*

sponse. Library usage has traditionally been measured by means of circulation records. These are the most universally-kept of all usage records and must be assigned a heavy weight. However, the provision of information is also an essential library function and the number of reference transactions is an important indicator of community response. If all libraries can agree on definitions and keep accurate records, the weight assigned in this category should be second only to circulation. The third element in measuring community response could take any one of three forms: registered borrowers, library visits, or program attendance. Although this author would prefer to use library visits (as recommended by UNESCO), relatively few American libraries maintain such records. More important, perhaps, is agreement among the libraries to use *one* of these and to keep accurate records. The number of registered borrowers was used by CIFC and Oklahoma. If we use 30 as the total weight for this category, the following values appear to be reasonable: circulation—15; reference transactions—10; registered borrowers (*or* library visits *or* program attendance)—5.

The proposed formula might be summarized as follows:

I. *Service Obligation* 35%

    a. Population of primary service area (25)
    b. Income disparity of population (5)
    c. Geographical size of primary service area (5)

II. *Library Provision* 35%

    a. Number of facilities (3)
    b. Square feet of usable space (2)
    c. Hours open per week (3)
    d. Size (FTE) of staff (18)
    e. Acquisitions budget (9)

III. *Community Response* 30%

    a. Circulation (15)
    b. Reference transactions (10)
    c. Registered borrowers (5)
       (*or* library visits *or* program attendance).

The elements in the proposed formula and the relative weights need to be analyzed and debated. Computer simulations need to be developed to test the effects of formula funding on public library performance. How would formula distribution differ from today's actual distribution? Would it be desirable as an ultimate goal? Or are there serious defects in the formula which should be remedied? Should there be a transition period between today's funding pattern and formula funding? How long should it be? These and many other questions will be addressed in a research project to be conducted by the Kent State University School of Library Science and Tantalus, Inc. during the 1984/85 academic year.

REFERENCES

1. *Public Library Funding and State Aid Eligibility and Distribution Criteria: A Partial Survey*, comp. by Ted Despres and Nancy Vincent. Columbus: State Library of Ohio, 1984, p. 1.

2. Brahm, Walter, "Commentary on the Library Laws of Ohio and Their Application" (1960) as cited in *Library Laws of Ohio in Force February 15, 1981*. Columbus: State Library of Ohio, 1981, p. ii.

3. *Ibid.*, pp. ii, 140. For more details on the early history, the 1932, 1933 and 1934 issues of the *Ohio Library Association News Bulletin* are very revealing, e.g., the court challenge to the constitutionality of the 1931 legislation and the corrective legislation in 1933.

4. For more details, see the Appendix "Public Library Finance," *Library Laws for Ohio . . ..* pp. 140-142.

5. *Ohio Revised Code* (hereafter cited as *ORC*) 5707.03, 5705.04.

6. *ORC* 5747.03 (2).

7. *ORC* 5747.49.

8. *Ibid.*

9. Am. Sub. H. B. 291, Sect. 128.

10. For further details, see the following works cited by Despres and Vincent in *Public Library Funding:* Ladenson, Alex. *Library Law and Legislation in the United States.* Metuchen, N.J.: Scarecrow Press, 1982; Mason, Marilyn Gell. *Public Library Finance.* Washington, D.C.: Office of Educational Research and Improvement, 1981 (ERIC: ED 223 262); Urban Libraries Council. *Survey of State Aid to Public Libraries, 1983-1984.* Chicago: Urban Libraries Council, 1983. Mason, incidentally, provides the following breakdown of sources of public library funding: local—82%; state—13%; federal—5%.

11. *Public Library Funding*, p. 4.

12. Caruthers, J. Kent, and Melvin Orwis, *Budgeting in Higher Education.* Washington, D.C.: American Association for Higher Education, 1979. (AAHE-ERIC/Higher Education Research Report No. 3.)

13. Gross, Francis M., *A Comparative Analysis of the Existing Budget Formulas Used for Justifying Budget Requests of Allocating Funds for the Operating Expenses of State-Supported Colleges and Universities.* Knoxville: University of Tennessee Office of Institutional Research, 1973.

14. *Formula Funding Mechanisms for State Support of Public Colleges and Universities in Michigan Based on a Study of Funding Mechanisms Across the Nation.* Lansing: Michigan State Department of Education, 1976.

A. Robert Rogers 43

15. "Ohio Board of Regents," *1983 Session Laws—Full Text (H. B. 291)*. Columbus: Banks-Baldwin, 1983 p. 5-214.

16. *Inter-Library Comparisons: Report to the British Library on a Feasibility Study by the Centre for Interfirm Comparison July 1977*. Colchester, Essex: The Centre for Interfirm Comparisons, 1977, p. 2.

17. Centre for Interfirm Comparison. *Inter-Library Comparisons: Pilot Comparison with Public Libraries*. London: British Library, 1981, p. 5.

18. *Ibid.*, p. 10.

19. *Ibid.*, p. 11.

20. *Ibid.*, Table 1.

21. *Ibid.*, Table 2.1

22. *Ibid.*

23. *Ibid.*, Table 2.3.

24. For a discussion of the major issues relating to national standards (including the revolution in professional thinking during the 1970s) see: Rolf, Robert H., "Standards for Public Libraries," *Library Trends* 31 (Summer 1982): 65-76.

25. *Standards for the Public Libraries of Ohio*. Columbus: Ohio Library Association, 1980, p. 4.

26. "Ohio Public Libraries: Supplemental Support," Testimony submitted to the Public Library Financing and Support Committee by Rachel Nelson, President, Ohio Library Association, February 15, 1984, p. 4.

27. De Prospo, Ernest, and others, *Performance Measures for Public Libraries*. Chicago: American Library Association, 1973, p. 31.

28. *Statewide Performance Guidelines for Oklahoma Public Libraries*. Rockville, MD: King Research, Inc., 1982, pp. i-iii and *Performance Measures for Oklahoma Public Libraries*. Oklahoma City: Oklahoma Department of Libraries, 1982, pp. i-iii.

29. *Statewide Performance Guidelines . . . .*, pp. 17-18.

30. "Avenues to Excellence: Illinois Library Association Standards for Public Library Services in Illinois," *Illinois Libraries* 65 (February 1983): 95-136.

31. Zweizig, Douglas, and Eleanor Jo Rodgers, *Output Measures for Public Libraries: A Manual of Standardized Procedures*. Chicago: American Library Association, 1982, pp. 1-91.

32. "Public Library Finance," *Library Laws of Ohio . . . .*, p. 140.

33. "Factors in Allocation of Intangibles Tax Funds," *Ohio Library Trustee* 22 (July 1970): 12-13, 20.

34. Winklepleck, Gordon, and John Rebenack, "Tax Allocation by Formula in Summit County," *Ohio Library Trustee* 41 (July 1979): 3-9.

35. "Guidelines for Equitable Distribution of the Local Situs Intangible Tax," *Ohio Library Trustee* 43 (July 1981): 3-10.

36. *Cuyahoga County Public Library Systems Allocation of Intangibles Tax Revenues*. Cleveland: Touche Ross & Co., 1983, *passim*.

37. "Intangibles Tax Collection and Distribution—County Summary—1982," *Statistics of Ohio Libraries*. Columbus: State Library of Ohio, 1983, pp. 6-7.

38. "Problems of Ohio Libraries," *The Ohio Long Range Program for Improvement of Library Services As Assisted by the Federal Library Services and Construction Act*. Columbus: State Library of Ohio, 1978, p. 17.

39. Blasingame, Ralph, *Survey of Ohio Libraries and the State Library Services: A Report to the State Library Board*. Columbus: State Library of Ohio, 1968, pp. 167-169.

40. Parsons, A. Chapman, "From the OLTA Desk," *Ohio Library Trustee* 31 (January 1969): 13.

41. *ORC* 3375.70-3375.82.

42. "Ohio Public Libraries: Supplemental Support . . . ." p. 7.

43. For a county-by-county breakdown, see Table II, "Counties Below Statewide Average of $12.29 in 1982," prepared by A. Robert Rogers for the Public Library Financing and Support Committee, November 1983.

Appendix -- Formula Calculations

For the sake of simplicity, let us assume a county called "X" which has three libraries call "A," "B," and "C."

A. Measures of Service Obligation   35%

1. Population (25)

Library A	150,000
Library B	700,000
Library C	50,000
Total	900,000

   Percentage share of total population

Library A	16.67%
Library B	77.78%
Library C	5.55%
Total	100.00%

   Reduced to assigned weight of 25, these percentages become:

Library A	4.17
Library B	19.44
Library C	1.39
Total	25.00

2. Income Disparity (5)

   Let us assume the 1980 census figures for income per household and the following system of inverse weighting: 0-$7,499--5; $7,500-$14,999--4; $15,000-$22,499--3; $22,500-$29,999--2; $30,000 and over--1.

Library A Family Incomes	(1) Weight Factor	(2) No. of Families	(1) x (2)
$ 0-$ 7,499	5	200	1,000
7,500- 14,999	4	1,000	4,000
15,000- 22,499	3	1,200	3,600
22,500- 30,000	2	5,000	10,000
30,000 and over	1	7,000	7,000
		14,400	25,600

   $$\frac{(1) \times (2)}{\text{Total \# Families}} = \frac{25,600}{14,400} = 1.78$$

Library A Family Incomes	(1) Weight Factor	(2) No. of Families	(1) x (2)
$ 0-$ 7,499	5	120,000	600,000
7,500- 14,999	4	50,000	200,000
15,000- 22,499	3	10,000	30,000
22,500- 30,000	2	5,000	10,000
30,000 and over	1	1,000	1,000
		186,000	841,000

   $$\frac{(1) \times (2)}{\text{Total \# Families}} = \frac{841,000}{186,000} = 4.52$$

Library C Family Incomes	(1) Weight Factor	(2) No. of Families	(1) x (2)
$ 0-$ 7,499	5	3,000	15,000
7,500- 14,999	4	4,000	16,000
15,000- 22,499	3	2,000	6,000
22,500- 30,000	2	1,000	2,000
30,000 and over	1	500	500
		10,500	39,500

$$\frac{(1) \times (2)}{\text{Total \# Families}} = \frac{39,500}{10,500} = 3.76$$

	(1) Tot # of Families	(2) Rank Factor	(3) % of Rank Factor	(3) x (1) Weighted Families	% of Weighted Families
Library A	14,400	1.78	17.69%	2,547.36	2.83%
Library B	186,000	4.52	44.93%	83,569.80	92.81%
Library C	10,500	3.76	37.38%	3,924.90	4.36%
Total in State	210,900	10.06	100.00%	90,042.06	100.00%

Reduced to formula weight of 5, these percentages become:

Library A	-	1.1415
Library B	-	4.6405
Library C	-	.2180
Total		5.000

3. Geographic Size of Primary Service Area (5)

Area in square miles

Library A	600
Lib... .ry B	125
Library C	5,375
Total	6,100

Percentage share of total area

Library A	9.836%
Library B	2.049%
Library C	88.115%
Total	100.000%

Reduced to the assigned weight of 5, these percentages become:

Library A	.4918
Library B	.10245
Library C	4.40575
Total	5.00000

For measures of service obligation, the summary becomes:

Library	Population	Income Disparity	Service Area	Total
A	4.17	.1415	.49180	4.80330
B	19.44	4.6405	.10245	24.18295
C	1.39	.2180	4.40575	6.01375
Total	25.00	5.0000	5.00000	35.00000

B. Measures of Library Provision   35%

1. Number of buildings or service outlets (3)

Library A	3
Library B	16
Library C	6
Total	25

Percentage share of total buildings or service outlets

Library A	12%
Library B	64%
Library C	24%
Total	100%

Reduced to the assigned weight of 3, these percentages become:

Library A	.36
Library B	1.92
Library C	.72
Total	3.00

2. Size of buildings or service outlets (2)

Library A	60,000 sq. ft. of usable space
Library B	320,000 sq. ft. of usable space
Library C	12,000 sq. ft. of usable space
Total	392,000 sq. ft. of usable space

Percentage share of total footage of usable space:

Library A	15.31%
Library B	81.63%
Library C	3.06%
Total	100.00%

Reduced to the assigned weight of 2, these percentages become:

Library A	.3062
Library B	1.6326
Library C	.0612
Total	2.0000

3. Hours open per week (3)

Library A	88
Library B	62
Library C	47
Total	197

    Percentage share of hours open per week

Library A	44.67%
Library B	31.47%
Library C	23.86%
Total	100.00%

    Reduced to the assigned weight of 3, these percentages become:

Library A	1.3401
Library B	.9441
Library C	.7158
Total	3.0000

4. Number (FTE) of staff (18)

Library A	90
Library B	280
Library C	15
Total	385

    Percentage share of staff

Library A	23.377%
Library B	72.727%
Library C	3.896%
Total	100.000%

    Reduced to assigned weight of 18, these percentages become:

Library A	4.20786
Library B	13.09086
Library C	.70128
Total	18.00000

5. Size of acquisitions budget (9)

Library A	$ 600,000
Library B	1,050,000
Library C	75,000
Total	$1,725,000

    Percentage share of collection

Library A	34.78%
Library B	60.87%
Library C	4.35%
Total	100.00%

Reduced to assigned weight of 9, these percentages become:

Library A	3.1302
Library B	5.4783
Library C	.3915
Total	9.0000

For measure of library provision, the summary becomes:

Library	No. Bldgs.	Sq. Ft.	Hours	Staff	Acq. Budget	Total
A	.36	.3062	1.3401	4.20786	3.1302	9.34436
B	1.92	1.6326	.9441	13.09086	5.4783	23.06586
C	.72	.0612	.7158	.70128	.3915	2.58978
Total	3.00	2.0000	3.0000	18.00000	9.0000	35.00000

C. Measures of Community Response

1. Circulation (15)   30%

Library A	2,100,000
Library B	5,600,000
Library C	550,000
Total	8,250,000

Percentage share of circulation

Library A	25.45%
Library B	67.88%
Library C	6.67%
Total	100.00%

Reduced to the assigned weight of 15, these percentages become:

Library A	3.8175
Library B	10.1820
Library C	1.0005
Total	15.0000

2. Reference transactions (10)

Library A	1,200,000
Library B	2,300,000
Library C	100,000
Total	3,600,000

Percentage share of reference transactions

Library A	33.33%
Library B	63.89%
Library C	2.78%
Total	100.00%

Reduced to the assigned weight of 10, these percentages become:

Library A	3.333
Library B	6.389
Library C	.278
Total	10.000

3. Registered borrowers (5)

Library A	105,000
Library B	210,000
Library C	20,000
Total	335,000

Percentage share of registered borrowers

Library A	31.34%
Library B	62.69%
Library C	5.97%
Total	100.00%

Reduced to the assigned weight of 5, these percentages become:

Library A	1.5670
Library B	3.1345
Library C	.2985
Total	5.0000

For measures of community response, the summary becomes:

Library	Circulation	Reference	Borrowers	Total
A	3.8175	3.333	1.5670	8.7175
B	10.1820	6.389	3.1345	19.7055
C	1.0005	.278	.2985	1.5770
Total	15.0000	10.000	5.0000	30.0000

The summary of all three groups of measure is:

Library	Service Obligation	Library Provision	Community Response	Total
A	4.80330	9.34436	8.7175	22.86516%
B	24.18295	23.06586	19.7055	66.95431%
C	6.01375	2.58978	1.5770	10.18053%
Total	35.00000	35.00000	30.0000	100.00000%

If $18,000,000 were available, the distribution would become:

Library A	$ 4,115,728.80
Library B	12,051,775.80
Library C	1,832,495.40
Total	$18,000,000.00

QWL in Academic/Research Libraries

Jean S. Decker

What is the Quality of your Work Life? Librarians, library educators, library directors, library boards have for years concentrated upon people as patrons to be served. Meanwhile, the people who serve have received scant attention as unique individuals. Work life is a large part of total life and should be made as satisfying as possible. What we do within any hour is significant, since every hour of life is precious. "Existing" in the workplace and "living" only on weekends and holidays are a wasteful compromise. Quality of work life is made of tangible and intangible elements, some small and some far-reaching. Each librarian, if asked, would define quality of work life in a special way according to his/her own needs.

WHO IS AFFECTED BY QWL?

Quality of work life in libraries is not a concern of just administrators, managers and supervisors. QWL should be on the agenda of all professional librarians regardless of level or specialization. Most librarians both "manage" and "are managed," "supervise" and "are supervised." The active forms of those verbs are spoken with pride while the passive forms are a turn-off. "Being managed" seems un-American because the words suggest loss of freedom and personal control. "Being supervised" is no improvement since visions of big brother or the Goodyear blimp hovering overhead float into the mind. Considering the negative, rebellious feelings these terms elicit, some new labels might serve us better.

Any good story needs conflict; a good library does not. On one side are workers at all levels who have varied goals and expectations, probably ill-defined and poorly communicated, and on the other side are institution goals and expectations equally ill-defined and poorly communicated. In the middle of this scenario are the managers, i.e., the librarians. Management has been defined as the

51

skill/art/science of getting things done through people. Thus defined, management takes many forms. For instance, the reference librarian is managed by the person who sets up the desk schedule. The same reference librarian manages a new arrival in the department who needs training. The subject bibliographer/selector is managed by a professor demanding a stronger collection. The selector manages (carefully) the acquisition librarian. The acquisition librarian is managed by selectors and he/she manages searchers, selectors, vendors, and accountants. The catalogers are managed by other catalogers, searchers, and selectors. The relationship between selector and acquisition librarian is a typical example of reciprocal management in action. The selector wants to get materials through the acquisition librarian and the acquisition librarian wants the selector to stop submitting requests for unwanted duplicates. Each is trying to get something done through the other.

HOW DO WE PREPARE?

Before entering the arena of crisscrossing goals, objectives, and expectations, the librarian desperately needs forewarning and forearming. The expanded expertise expected of academic/research librarians can no longer be guaranteed within a 36-hour program. Once upon a time, knowing something about every discipline and its major resources; reading three or four foreign languages at least well enough to translate titles, content pages, and relevant descriptions; knowing the cataloging code; and understanding whatever records served to control collections were the basic qualifications expected of a research librarian. Now there is more. The need to know still another cataloging code, how to retrieve bibliographic information stored in computers, how to operate terminals connected to multiple databases, standards for input, standards for conversion projects, personal computer applications, preservation techniques, automated systems for all processes, etc., are overloading the library school curriculum. There's no room for personnel management.

Courses in management and interpersonal relationships are standard elements in a librarian's preparation. Management courses include many important subjects: allocation of resources, staffing, budget preparation, system evaluation, report writing, goal setting, community relations, fund raising, and similar topics of concern to library directors, but scant attention is paid to the living, breathing human beings who do the work in our libraries. Courses in interpersonal relationships generally look to patron/librarian relationships, not to worker/manager relationships. Why personnel management has been overlooked is guesswork. Perhaps managing and supervising do not seem "scholarly." They may be so tightly associated with business and moneymaking as to put them outside a "service" profession. They may be looked upon as an application of common sense unworthy of serious study. *NOT SO*. Managing and supervising are difficult art forms that librarians need to master. If library schools cannot provide the essentials in these areas, the world's best information seekers and finders, i.e., librarians, must educate themselves. The academic/research librarian has unending resources at hand, not necessarily in library literature, but in the literature of business and management, of psychology, of sociology, of education, and of any field in which employed people matter. By selecting the ideas that are applicable and transferable to a library's personnel situation, any librarian can find ways to sharpen managerial skills.

Accountability is riding high. As the tax dollar is stretched like taffy, the oft-repeated questions are: "Am I getting my money's worth?", "What or who can be cut out?" and "How can more be done for less?" With the steady shriveling of staffs, the remaining people are becoming a greater and greater resource.

WHY IS QWL IMPORTANT?

The obvious, and simplistic, answer is that happy satisfied workers are productive, they relate well to patrons and co-workers, and they are strong contributors to an institution's growth and improvement. Quality of work life programs improve the aspects of the work situation that promote a more satisfying work life. Some specifics will be discussed later.

There is a common misconception that workers should be happy if they receive a good paycheck. Money may be the primary need at some point but it is frequently displaced by other needs. Maslow, in setting forth his hierarchy of needs, pointed out the fluid nature of the hierarchy. As one need is met, others take precedence over it. When a librarian first seeks a job, *physiological* needs, such as a warm house, food, and a car that runs may be at the top of the list.

The quality of work life can be quite bad at this point and still be acceptable if the pay is good. Once the physiological needs are satisfied, the *security* need may move to the top spot. Assuming that security equals hanging on to the job, meeting the requirements that lead to permanent status becomes a high priority. The quality of work life is now measured by a different scale. To what extent does work life include opportunities to meet the prescribed requirements? Considering tenure track expectations and the scarcity of released time, we may have encountered a conflict between worker goals and institution goals. If the requirements can be met and the security need is satisfied, *social* needs may take over as number one in the hierarchy. Work life has an extensive social side. It may be a large part of a librarian's social life. Friends get together for lunch and breaks. Cards and a free lunch mark your birthday. If you are ill, concern is expressed. Your problems and your joys bring appropriate reactions from co-workers. Since socializing takes time, the potential for another conflict between worker and institution goals exists. Important though it is to the worker, socializing time may be perceived by the institution as time wasted. Evidence indicates that the improvement in morale and community feeling fostered by social time is time well spent.

The last two needs, i.e., 4 and 5, are more individualistic and are seldom acknowledged in library organizations. The *ego* need for recognition, prestige, appreciation and credit frequently goes unrecognized and unfilled. Closely linked to ego need is the need for *self-fulfillment*. Workers have a right to expect "psyche income" along with monetary income. Workers have talents that remain untapped and unused. Policies relevant to the last two needs are the ripest for major upgrading.

The results of a study on what workers considered important about their jobs were reported in the April 1984 issue of *Supervisory Management*. The top five choices of white collar workers were:

1. Chance to do interesting work.
2. Chance for a raise.
3. Chance to do quality work.
4. Chance for promotion.
5. Getting along with co-workers.

One and three grow out of the need to use our abilities to their fullest; two and four are standard devices for rewarding superior performance; and five enhances the social side of work.

WHAT FACTORS DETERMINE
THE QUALITY OF WORK LIFE?

It is no great mystery. All people, librarians included, need and find satisfaction in a work life which encourages self-respect and affords opportunities for growth and development. Quality of work life can be improved by changed attitudes, awareness, and sensitivity, or by a specific plan of action. A QWL plan does not have to be system-wide. It can be a department project, a section goal, or one person changing his/her management style. It can start anywhere, with anyone. A brief look at a couple of broad areas, communication and ergonomics, may start ideas germinating.

Communication is a key ingredient in quality of work life. The success or failure of training, appraisals, staff meetings, participative management, interpersonal relationships, management style, discipline, motivation, and that all-important category of general information dissemination can be traced to the quality of written and oral communication.

The last category is a heavyweight. People may not like the content of the message, but they want to know what *is* going on and what *will be* going on. Information dissemination within an organization is a sensitive and critical area. Information, where it comes from, who gets it and by what route, has an assigned status rating. There is no classification table by which we can calculate the status rating for any given piece of information, but it does exist. Knowing why the electricians are knocking holes in the wall has one rating, whereas knowing whether or not the Friday after Thanksgiving will be declared a holiday has another rating. Managers are apt to rely on "the need to know" as a distribution policy. This leaves many interested people guessing and assuming the worst. Letting information spread by way of the grapevine invites distortion of the facts. Those who are affected by decisions are incensed that they were not told and the resulting bruised ego devalues the quality of that person's work life. Admittedly, information has to be selectively and effectively disseminated, but little that goes on in a library is "top secret." The important point is that the more the staff knows, the more they feel a part of the action. In a practical sense, information allows each librarian to appreciate how decisions and procedures in one section will affect other operations. Timely distribution of information allows reaction and valuable feedback while opening up opportunities for self-fulfillment.

Before touching on other activities partly or wholly dependent on communication, let's consider what makes good communication possible. The usual goal is to transfer information (the message) to a reader, a viewer, or a listener.

The message has to be in a form that is intelligible to the receiver whether the sender is talking, writing, or listening. An oral presentation must take into account that we comprehend complexities less well orally than visually. Redundancy that works well in a speech may come out as verbosity when the speech is printed. The message in a speech that is written and read may wing its way overhead and out the door. Listening is also a message mover. Body language can say, "That's fascinating, exciting; I don't agree; I don't understand; you wouldn't dare; you're boring me."

When we set out to communicate, we expect to be understood. Well, usually. What goes wrong? The first major obstacle is words and their definitions. Your definition may not be my definition. Someone has calculated that the 500 most used words have 14,000 definitions. A second obstacle is attitude. The receiver may disagree with the message, dislike the sender, hate the medium carrying the message, or dread the consequences. A third obstacle is overload, a common problem for new people learning a new system. The capacity to assimilate new information is variable and proper pacing will minimize frustration. A fourth obstacle is distractions in the form of noise, movement, or interruptions. The fifth obstacle is common to orally transmitted information. Distortion of a message passed through a long chain can be funny or disastrous. Since communication is a two-way exchange, the receiver can encounter the same obstacles as the sender plus a couple more. Lack of attention or concentration catches us with half the message or none of it. A sender who provides no opportunity for feedback can be unaware of communication breakdown until a problem surfaces. A good climate for productive exchange is based upon the right attitude, patient listening, objectivity, and a real desire to understand.

Remembering a few rules can make you a better communicator:

1. Decide what the message is, what you want the receiver to retain, and what behavior you wish to shape.
2. Know your audience or readership. Keep in mind their interests, level of experience, and their aspirations.
3. Select the right time and place to communicate.
4. Choose the vehicle that best carries the message.
5. Encourage feedback and be ready to listen.

Good training is based upon good communication. Together they contribute to good QWL. The librarian approaching a new job, even in an old setting, has to prove to herself/himself that he/she can handle the new challenge. The sooner procedures are known and independent work is possible, the sooner that person's self-concept is strengthened and satisfaction is experienced. Training is not a one-time shot. It should be a continuous process which augments a person's participation, readiness for change and opportunities for self-improvement. Well defined procedures and clearly written manuals spare the newcomer confusion and embarrasment.

Appraisals can be a difficult communication task. Evaluation is a very serious matter in a librarian's work life. In the natural course of events, a superior librarian is rarely complimented, praised, or shown any appreciation. Likewise, administrators are prone to let a mediocre performance continue rather than face up to an encounter which will be emotionally upsetting or trying. In either case, the librarian often works in a vacuum devoid of feedback. A good communicator and sensitive supervisor does not let this condition develop. There are solutions. Although monetary rewards are not available, recognition in the form of more responsibility, a committee assignment, a promotion, a certificate of merit, a pat on the back or a compliment are usually possible. Mediocre performance may spring from inadequate training, wrong assumptions about prior preparation, lack of resources, or a mismatch of worker and job requirements. An honest discussion focusing on the work and not the person may clear up a long-standing problem.

Participative management and concern for quality of work life have a chicken/egg relationship. Participative management and QWL were born when efforts to find out why workers were unhappy and dissatisfied with work life produced comments such as, "I have no part in setting goals," "No one listens to my ideas even though I have years of experience in this work," "I have no chance to develop leadership skills," "I want to have some input when decisions are made," "I feel de-humanized," and "I have the closest view of the situation and understand the problem."

Dr. Nancy Dixon of the University of Texas at Austin lists "four major elements in participative management: an information system that provides timely feedback on organizational performance, systematic representation of employees at all levels, alignment around a vision that is shared by all, and the organizational leaders' belief in the creativity and responsibility of employees."[1] Obviously, good communication is a vital factor in the success of participative management.

Another key ingredient in quality work life is ergonomics. A worker feels that his/her worth is recognized when there are signs that a supervisor is concerned about safety, esthetics, comfort, noise, and the quality of equipment. There have been discussions and tests to measure the effects of radiation emitted by video display terminals. Since shields have been developed to minimize any danger, failure to purchase such shields may be seen as a disregard for worker safety. Drafty work areas, poor lighting, inadequate maintenance or copiers that seldom work send signals to workers that the institution cares little about their work or them as individuals.

CONCLUSION

Although the expression, "People are our greatest asset" is commonly heard, use of the word "asset" in this context is debatable. As Drucker points out, "Asset is by definition something one can sell and something that has value when a company goes into liquidation. But a company does not own people."[2] The idea that people are essential to their organizations is valid, however. That's particularly true of library systems, for a library is only as good as its staff. As the patron has a right to quality service from the librarian, so the librarian has a right to a quality work life.

REFERENCES

1. Dixon, Nancy, "'Participative Management': It's Not As Simple As It Seems," *Supervisory Mangement,* 29 (December, 1984), 2-8.

2. Drucker, Peter F., "Management: Tasks, Responsibilities, Practices," New York: Harper & Row, 1974, p. 308.

Commas, Colons, and Parentheses: The International Standardization of Serials Holdings Statements

Marjorie E. Bloss

For many years, librarians and non-librarians alike have struggled to define a serial and to distinguish it from other entities. The results run the gamut from the extensive definition found in *Anglo-American Cataloguing Rules,* 2nd edition (*AACR2*) to ones somewhat more circumlocutious like the following which appeared recently in a local university newspaper: "A monograph is any library item which is not a periodical."[1] While we who work with serials continuously are more likely to rely on the definition found in *AACR*2, considerable sympathy lies with those whose groping results in elusive definitions such as the one quoted above. For these individuals in particular, the definition of a serial is a moot point. Much more important are questions like: "Does the library own the title and issue I want?; Where is it?; and, When can I use it?" The first of these questions is at the heart of this paper for unless users can determine what issues, numbers, volumes, years, etc., of a serial title are held in a library, the last two questions are irrelevant.

BACKGROUND

Always a cornerstone of a library's collection, serials have increased dramatically in importance in the 20th century due to the explosion of scientific research. Not only has the number of serial titles proliferated at a rate that would put hamsters to shame, but subscription prices have continued upward at alarming speed. These trends have raised the frustration level of both librarians and library users: the former when their library lacks a particular title or volume of that title; the latter when they request a title only to be told of its unavailability. The truth of the matter becomes quickly apparent: no one library can own all serial titles or all issues of all titles. As a

59

result, libraries have become more and more dependent on one another for supplementing the gaps in their own collections.

A number of important serial-related activities have occurred during the past ten or so years which have facilitated the sharing not only of bibliographic data but of actual materials. Among the major events are the acceptance of the MARC-S format; the building of the CONSER data base; the work of ISDS and NSDP; the creation of a national standard for the display of serial holdings statements, and most recently, the development of a separate MARC format for the storage of those holdings. Although the United States has been at the forefront of a number of these activities, other countries have similar concerns and interests equaling our own.

One characteristic of serials is the equal importance of bibliographic information and holdings data. If the bibliographic data can be likened to the right arm of the serial organism then undisputedly the holdings information represents the left. Unfortunately, a double entendre is appropriate here, for until fairly recently, holdings statements have indeed been left . . . left behind in librarians' efforts of standardization.

Even so, methods of representing serial holdings data have existed locally for many years. The lack of uniformity in the display of this information on both national and international fronts, however, has resulted in a dense thicket of punctuation, symbols and abbreviations. The standardization of the serials bibliographic record coupled with the increased flexibility in data manipulation has emphasized the need for uniformity in the display of holdings information. Interestingly, this need became most apparent with the proliferation of union lists of serials which resulted from the increased ability of libraries to share bibliographic data. The current (as of this writing) American National Standards Institute's *Standard on Serials Holdings Statements at the Summary Level,* Z39.42-1980 acknowledged its origins as an outgrowth of the CONSER Project.[2] On the international scene, the story is very similar.

INTERNATIONAL DEVELOPMENTS
IN THE STANDARDIZATION
OF HOLDINGS STATEMENTS

Union lists of serials are viewed as a method of informing users not only of what titles are held in two or more (usually) independent libraries or institutions, but also of the extent of retention of those titles. The end to these means is resource sharing: permitting users to have access to serials not found in their own libraries. A union list of serials, therefore, can be viewed as an embodiment of two of the International Federation of Library Associations and Institutions's (IFLA) goals: Universal Bibliographic Control (UBC), and the Universal Availability of Publications (UAP). Underlying both of these programs is the need for the standardization of both bibliographic and holdings data. Without it, there would be no uniformity in the way these pieces of information are represented. This in turn would result in extensive problems when attempting to identify a title and its respective parts for resource sharing purposes.

In 1979 an IFLA/UNESCO grant to recommend guidelines for the compilation of union catalogues of serials was accepted by Jean Whiffin. Her working document entitled *Guidelines for Union Catalogues of Serials*[3] was analyzed in 1982 by an Ad Hoc Group on the Compilation of Union Catalogues of Serials which drew its representation from the International Serials Data System International Center, the Nordisk Samkatalog over Periodika (NOSP), the IFLA International Office for UBC, and members of IFLA's Section on Serial Publications. (Miss Whiffin's working document has been published by The Haworth Press as: *Union Catalogues of Serials: Guidelines for Creation and Maintenance, with Recommended Standards for Bibliographic and Holdings Control.*)[4] The Ad Hoc Group extracted those pieces of information deemed essential for the final document. This document, *Guidelines for the Compilation of Union Catalogues of Serials*[5] was published in late 1982 in order to fulfill the charge of the IFLA/UNESCO contract.

As a result of her work, Miss Whiffin presented to the IFLA Section on Serial Publications some twenty recommendations stemming from her analysis. Among them was a desire for some mechanism standardizing the display of serial holdings statements at the summary level. It had soon become apparent that on an international scale no guidelines, let alone standards, existed concerning the representation of holdings statements. The Ad Hoc Group had suggested that the IFLA Section on Serial Publications address the issue at the 1982 annual IFLA Conference. The Section felt it important that a standard be issued by the International Standard Organization's Technical Committee 46 (ISO TC 46), the international counterpart to the United States' National Information Standards Organization (NISO) Z39. Subsequently, a project proposal to prepare a working document as a starting point for a future standard for serial holdings statements was accepted by the IFLA Professional Board. The goals of this project are as follows:

1. To analyze at the national and international levels both the current state of the art and plans for the future development of standardized serial holdings statements.
2. To provide a framework for reporting serial holdings statements at the summarized condensed level (i.e., holdings expressed at the primary or most inclusive level of a serial's scheme of enumeration and/or chronology).
3. To provide ISO TC 46 with a working paper from which the Technical Committee can develop an international standard on holdings statements.

Although serial holdings statements are the primary focus of this project, the intent is to develop a framework by which serial holdings at the detailed level and of other materials could be represented as well. In early 1983, I was asked by Gunter Franzmeier, Chairperson, and Ross M. Bourne, Secretary of the IFLA Section on Serial Publications to analyze those standards or national practices dealing with serial holdings statements either currently in use or under development.

METHODOLOGY

In early 1983, Ross M. Bourne wrote on my behalf to the national libraries that comprise the membership of the Conference of National Libraries. In his letter, he requested that any information pertaining to the national standards or practices concerning the formatting of serial holdings statements be forwarded to me. As a result of his letter, 35 responses were received.[6] The contents of these responses varied greatly. In some cases, official standards were received; in other cases, general practices which had been established that could easily be considered as *de facto* standards were described; in yet other cases, countries reported that no standards or general practices existed.

The information received was then analyzed according to a number of different questions. Did the country have an established standard, or did it follow long-standing practices? What was the order of enumeration and chronology data? Were captions used? What punctuation, symbols, or abbreviations were used? How were gaps in holdings, incomplete volumes, microforms, notes pertaining to local policies, numbering irregularities and other variations in publication handled?

In many cases, no explanatory documentation was forwarded concerning the order of data elements or punctuation and symbols in a country's holdings statement. As a result, much of the analysis was based on an interpretation of the holdings statement itself rather than on some written explanation that could be used along with it. Frequently, follow-up letters were written to the responding libraries requesting clarification of the holdings data that had been submitted. On occasion, no response from those libraries was received. If this was the case, assumptions were made as best they could based on the documentation in hand.

The resulting document, the *Recommendations for Serial Holdings Statements at the Summarized Condensed Level,*[7] was reviewed by the IFLA Section on Serial Publications, its Working Group on Union Catalogues of Serials, and several observers at the 1984 IFLA Conference in Nairobi. A consensus was reached concerning its recommendations and the final draft will be submitted to ISO TC 46. In addition, plans are being made to have it published by the International Office for UBC. Some of the major conclusions of the analysis and the resulting recommendations found in the Working Paper will now be discussed.

BASIC CONCEPTS

Along with the questions used for analysis which were identified above, six more concepts form the basis for the recommendations found in the Working Paper. These are the following:

1. The impetus for this document grew out of a need for the standardization of the display of serial holdings statements as found in union lists of serials. In the vast majority of cases, the holdings statements found in these lists are formatted at the summarized level rather than at a detailed, issue-specific level. This was most certainly the case in the examples forwarded by the institutions responding to the request for serials holdings information. As a result, holdings statements at the summarized level have been the focus of this Working Paper. Even so, the recommendations in this document have been made with the knowledge that in the future they may include or influence holdings statements at a more detailed level. The application of these recommendations should be able to be extended to detailed holdings statements with relative ease.

If a standard for detailed holdings is desirable, it would be preferable to combine in a single standard the guidelines for holdings statements at both the detailed and summary levels rather than to have two separate standards. A decision should be made early on in ISO TC 46's deliberations either to have one standard covering both detailed and summary holdings or to have separate standards for each reporting level.

2. The emphasis of this working paper is on the display of serial holdings statements at the summarized level rather than the machine storage of this information. For developing nations and those countries attempting to standardize holdings data, display is the immediate concern. There is little doubt, however, that the need for an international standard for storing holdings statements in machine readable form will soon be recognized.

3. Because this is a working paper rather than a finalized standard, options have been included where two or more equally valid representations of a holdings statement exist. Although ISO TC 46 may eventually wish to select one option over another, the inclusion of different representations of the same information for consideration at this time was deemed important. In this way, different approaches to a single situation are quickly apparent and available for evaluation.

4. There should be similarity in the formatting of the bibliographic representation of a title's enumeration and chronology data with that of a holdings statement if at all possible. Consistency in these areas will greatly aid the user in the interpretation of both the bibliographic and holdings data.

5. The holdings statement should be kept as simple and uncluttered as possible yet should aid the user in determining what truly is owned by the institution. Punctuation marks, symbols, and explanatory notes should be functional and precise.

6. Any coding which is to serve as a basis for a computer sort (e.g., codes representing whether or not a title is currently received, whether or not a title is permanently retained, etc.) should not be included in the holdings statement itself. This does not preclude, however, carrying this information in machine-readable formats.

Some of the Working Paper's more specific recommendations will now be detailed.

RECOMMENDATIONS FOUND
IN THE WORKING PAPER

As was stated earlier, 35 responses were received to the request for information on national practices concerning serial holdings practices. Of these 35, only two—the United Kingdom and the United States—could point to established standards on serial holdings statements. Two countries were evaluating these two standards for their own use. Five indicated that they were basing their holdings on Area 3 of the ISBD(S) which deals with a serial's enumeration and chronology data. The remaining countries based their holdings on long standing national practices which, needless to say, differed and conflicted from one nation to another.

The order in which the enumeration and chronology data of a holdings statement should be displayed was, quite naturally, of major concern. Of the countries who responded to this question (or who formatted holdings statements at all), 10 displayed holdings as strings of enumeration followed by strings of chronology.

EXAMPLE:

Vol. 1,3,5-8,10-   1960,1962,1964-1967,1969-

Twenty nations displayed serial holdings in the order of enumeration followed immediately by its corresponding chronology.

EXAMPLE:

Vol. 1(1960),3(1962),5(1964)-8(1967),10(1969)-

(The punctuation separating the enumeration from the chronology varied depending on the overall scheme of punctuation and symbols used by the reporting country.)

Although the recommendations in the Working Paper indicate that holdings statements shall be independent of any cataloging code or concepts found in cataloging, an attempt was made to conform to the framework found in ISBD(S), Area 3. This was done for two reasons. First, ISBD(S) has been accepted by much of the library community. Second, even though ISBD(S) does not include all of the elements essential for the representation of a holdings statement, a number of libraries which responded to this project indicated that they planned to base holdings statements according to ISBD(S). As a result, the second example above reflecting enumeration followed immediately by its corresponding chronology was the recommendation made concerning the order of enumeration and chronology. Determining the punctuation and symbols to be used with a serials holdings statement was no easy matter. Three patterns of punctuation became evident after an analysis of the submitted data. The first followed the examples found in what we consider to be more traditional union lists like the *Union List of Serials in the United States and Canada*. The second patterned itself after the punctuation found in Area 3 of the ISBD(S). The third group of punctuation found its basis in the holdings statements of East Germany, West Germany, Hungary and Czechoslovakia. Most notable in this scheme are the uses of a comma separating first and second order designations (i.e., 2,10 represents volume 2, number 10), and a semicolon indicating gaps in a library's holdings (i.e., 2;4;6 is interpreted as the library holds volumes 2, 4, and 6 and lacks volumes 3 and 5).

As with the order of enumeration and chronology, the decision was made to base the punctuation used in holdings statements on ISBD(S). Needless to say, punctuation had to be augmented to represent gaps in holdings (a comma); a delimiter between different levels either of enumeration or chronology (a colon); and a method of indicating different physical formats when represented in one holdings statement (a second function of the equal sign).

OPTIONS FOUND IN THE WORKING PAPER

In the vast number of cases, the recording of serials holdings statements is a straightforward activity. Because serials are erratic creatures in their bibliographic habits, however, it comes as no surprise that the rules governing the representation of their holdings require flexibility. The inclusion of options in the Working Paper satisfied several needs. First of all, it addresses the fact that there isn't always one way and one way only to represent the same piece of information. Equally valid methods can co-exist. Second, the inclusion of options serves to heighten ISO TC 46's awareness of these differences. Finally, if ISO TC 46 does wish to mandate one method over another for representing certain aspects of serials holdings, it can do so from knowledge rather than by omission. Some of these major options found in the Working Paper will now be examined.

A basic premise of the Working Paper is that serial holdings statements shall be reported at the summarized rather than the detailed level. When the Working Paper was discussed at the 1984 IFLA Conference, there was further discussion as to how summarized was summarized. This question was raised especially in conjunction with a library reporting a number of gaps in the holdings of a particular title. The concern focused on the cost of maintaining the many thousands of these extensive holdings statements in a large file. A Precision Code as defined in the British Holdings Standard[8] was introduced as an optional data element to allow institutions the alternative of recording holdings data as concisely as possible. The Precision Codes enable holdings statements to be represented without identifying each gap in a holding. Five coded values are defined and are used to represent the percentage of the title held in the institution rather than published.

CODE VALUE	*DEFINITION*
1	95% and above of the holdings maintained
2	75% to less than 95%
3	50% to less than 75%
4	Less than 50%
5	Percentage accuracy of holdings not known.

A holdings statement could be represented in one of two ways. Either:

Vol. 2(1969)-3(1970),6(1973)-8(1975),10(1979)-

or it could be reduced to

Vol. 2(1969)-   (with a Precision Code of 3)

While the Precision Code offers the option of consolidating the information in a holdings statement, two other options allow for holdings statements that are almost detailed in level. The first of these permits the user to record first and second order designators (volumes and issues; years and months) if holdings begin or end in the middle of a volume. A combination of volumes and issues, however, should not be included in the middle of a summarized holdings statement.

EXAMPLE: (A publication issued monthly)

   Vol. 3:no. 2(1950:2)-10(1957),12(1959)-15:4(1962:4)
                    but not
   Vol. 3:no. 2(1950:2)-10:8(1957:9),12:5(1959:5)-15:4(1962:4)
           or, if no second order used at all
   Vol. 3(1950)-10(1957),12(1959)-15(1962)
           or, if a Precision Code were used
   Vol. 3(1950)-   (with a Precision Code of 1)

The second option permits the user to record second order designators if the title is deemed so important to the collection that issue-
specific data are needed. This is very much a value judgement on the
part of the reporting library and should be used sparingly on a case-
by-case basis.

A second basic premise of the Working Paper is that enumeration
and chronology data in a holdings statement shall reflect those
pieces of information that are represented on the publication itself.
If no enumeration is included on the piece, none shall appear in the
holdings statement. The same holds true for chronology data. An
exception has been made for non-Christian era dates. Ordinarily,
these are to be recorded as they appear on the publication without
conversion. If the reporting library wishes, however, it may add a
converted date in square brackets.

The use of local notes is another option presented in the Working
Paper. These notes permit the user to supplement or in certain cases
to replace enumeration and chronology data with a verbal description of the holdings information. If they are used, local notes shall
be institution specific, assisting the user in the interpretation of a
holdings statement. Information relating to the bibliographic description of a serial (such as changes in a serial's numbering sequence of discontinuity in the enumeration pattern) shall not be
recorded in this data element. Such information should be regarded
as bibliographic data and should be reflected in the bibliographic information itself. Examples of local notes include: information about
a library's retention policy; local access restrictions; status of physical condition; and, information pertaining to the physical medium
of the serial held.

This last use of local notes addresses a very controversial bibliographic issue, namely the "correct" method for handling reproductions (be they microforms or reprints) of the originally published title. Traditionally in a union list of serials, holdings statements for different physical formats of the same title have been linked to one bibliographic description, usually that of the original form of publication or production. More recently, some cataloging codes in general and *AACR2* in particular call for a separate bibliographic description and, therefore, cataloging record for each physical format. While this second method may be more accurate for bibliographic control or for a serials check-in record, the first may be more conducive to a union list of serials. Those with large serial files may find it advantageous to relinquish some degree of bibliographic accuracy in favor of a more concise and economical listing of titles. Although it is beyond the scope of the Working Paper to indicate a preference for one method over the other, options have been included giving users local autonomy in making this decision.

If separate bibliographic records are used for each physical format, a local note shall be included in the holdings statement informing the user to consult other relevant bibliographic records of the same title for additional information.

EXAMPLE:

(On the paper copy record):
  Vol. 1(1895)-40(1934)   See other record for microfilm holdings.
(On the microfilm record):
  Vol. 41(1935)-   See other record for paper copy holdings.

When local policy calls for using one bibliographic record for all physical formats of a single title, local notes shall be used to identify which units are held in what physical format. One of two methods may be employed when using the same bibliographic record for holdings in different physical formats. The first and preferred way is to create a separate string of holdings for each physical format owned by the library under one bibliographic description. A library holding the same title in paper copy, microfilm, and microfiche would therefore, display three separate holdings statements.

EXAMPLE:

Title ABC
Library G   Vol. 1(1895)-40(1934) = Paper copy
Library G   Vol. 35(1930)-40(1934) = Microfilm
Library G   Vol. 41(1935)-   = Microfiche

The second method would display the holdings first in one composite statement after which would come a breakdown of specific holdings for each physical format listed in chronological order.

EXAMPLE:

Title ABC
Library G Vol. 1(1895)- 1(1895)-40(1934) = Paper copy.
35(1930)-40(1934) = Microfilm. 41(1935)- = Microfiche.

Of course there is yet another method of reporting holdings in different physical formats which skirts the issue altogether. Some libraries may not wish to specify different physical formats at all and may simply report their holdings as:

Vol. 1(1895)-

CONCLUSION

These, then are some of the major recommendations found in the *Recommendations for Serial Holdings Statements at the Summarized Condensed Level* that will be submitted to ISO TC 46. In it are many features found in the two existing standards on serial holdings statements from the United Kingdom and the United States as well as elements found in common from the holdings of other nations. Many changes can occur between the time the Working Paper is submitted to ISO TC 46 and its acceptance. Hopefully, any revisions or additions will be made expeditiously so the recording and displaying of serial holdings statements can reach the same level of international uniformity as that of serials bibliographic data.

REFERENCES

1. "Library Renovated," *Technology News,* 117 (October 1, 1984):1.
2. *American National Standard for Serial Holdings Statements at the Summary Level* (ANSI Z39.42-1980). New York: American National Standards Institute, 1980.

3. Whiffin, Jean. *Guidelines for Union Catalogues of Serials.* Victoria, British Columbia, 1981.

4. Whiffin, Jean. *Union Catalogues of Serials: Guidelines for Creation and Maintenance, with Recommended Standards for Bibliographic and Holdings Control.* New York: The Haworth Press, 1983.

5. *Guidelines for the Compilation of Union Catalogues of Serials.* Paris: Unesco, IFLA, 1982.

6. The national libraries who responded to the call for information on serial holdings statements are the following: Australia, Austria, Belgium, Czechoslovakia, Denmark, Finland, France, East Germany, West Germany, Greece, Guyana, Hungary, Iceland, India, Indonesia, Ireland, Italy, Japan, Malaysia, New Zealand, Norway, People's Republic of China, Peru, Republic of South Africa, Singapore, Soviet Union, Sri Lanka, Sweden, Taiwan, Tanzania, Thailand, Turkey, United Kingdom, United States, Zambia.

7. Bloss, Marjorie E. *Recommendations for Serial Holdings Statements at the Summarized Condensed Level.* Prepared for the IFLA section on serial publications. Chicago: 1983 [i.e., 1984].

8. *Specifications for Serials Holdings Statements for Libraries and Documentation Centres* (BS 5999:1980). London: British Standards Institution, 1980.

The Serials-Centered Library

Barbara P. Pinzelik

AN IMPROBABLE HISTORY

The first monograph was received in the Gramwell Public Library on June 4, 1896. Its source was unknown, but it was undoubtedly a gift from one of the numerous library benefactors. "What am I supposed to do with this?" grumbled Lucinda Darvis, the ill-tempered but conscientious cataloger. "Here's a new title with no volume or part numbers indicated. And look how small it is. How can it be shelved? It will be lost among the neat rows of library materials." The piece sat on her desk for weeks, until a few more monographs trickled in, and articles began appearing in the sparse library literature dealing with the difficulty of handling this new form.

This same situation had been happening in libraries throughout the world, as the monograph slowly began to appear. Until then, the serial was the form of recorded knowledge, beginning with the Egyptian *Periodical of the Dead,* left in tombs as a guide to the deceased. The early writers and scholars thought of knowledge as a continuum. The steady flow of manuscripts, numbered and dated by the scholars who realized the importance of maintaining this continuum, became known as "periodicals" from the Greek work "πεpιoδikos" meaning "coming round at certain intervals." Later, in the Roman Empire they were known as "serials" from the Latin word for "row" or "chain."

One of the major works of the early period, reflecting the sacred writings of the Christian religion, was called *The Periodical.* Written over many years by various authors, some unknown, it is a well-known example of the form. With the invention of moveable type, this was the first periodical to be printed. A major impact on scholarship and the rapid development of libraries was the result.

The monastic and the early university libraries contained many serials manuscripts, which consisted of learned writings as well as

73

chronicles of the times. It was usually the custom to chain these serials to their stations. With the invention of the printed serial, these restrictions fell into disrepute. The appearance of libraries now began to evolve into the nineteenth-century model—rows of neatly and similarly bound journals.

The emergence of the monograph took place in the mid-seventeenth century. Initially rare, these titles found their way into the larger university and national libraries. Because librarianship did not really develop until the nineteenth century, the significance of this difference in form was not grasped by "keepers of periodicals," and they were treated much the same as the serials.

However, with the development of librarianship and the emerging popularity of the monograph as a bibliographic form, libraries all over the world began to experience what the Gramwell public library and its cataloger were about to undergo.

SERIALS REALITY

The above narrative, an exercise in library science fiction, ignores 5000 years of intellectual history but allows one to speculate on the way serials are treated in libraries. How different would libraries be if the serial had developed before the monograph? For decades, library practice has seemed to treat serials like unruly monographs. It is interesting to imagine what libraries would be like if the serial had pre-dated the monograph.

Those of us who call ourselves serials librarians believe that our work is the most demanding, exacting, and undervalued of all library specialties. A harmless but interesting form of retaliation for lack of appreciation might be to imagine what libraries would be like if the serial were the pre-eminent form. To begin, let us summarize some of the major differences between library treatment of serials and monographs.

Acquisitions

Until the past 20-30 years, there were few bibliographic aids for selecting and acquisition of serials. It is still preferable for specialists to deal with serials selection and ordering in large libraries. One difficulty with selection, as pointed out by Osborn, is that "at least four-fifths of all serials are not trade publications . . . They can therefore be more elusive . . ."[1]

Serials selection has a significant effect on a library's budget and its space allocation. Those making such decisions, if they do it properly, need the skills of a prophet, the ability of a detective, and the daring of a gambler. The same skills are needed to review the collection, eliminating titles no longer meeting the mission of the library. An area of acquisitions often understaffed is the serials check-in unit. Overworked and overwhelmed by the quantity, variety, and complexity of the daily influx of serials, check-in clerks usually have little time, after processing the day's mail, to begin the laborious process of claiming. Lack of persistence reduces the likelihood of success, consequently serials clerks become discouraged and the process can become self-defeating.

A larger and more aggressive serials acquisitions staff is needed to solve the problem. If serials had appeared before monographs in libraries, a much larger portion of the staff would probably be involved in serials check-in and claiming, with a much greater success rate.

Cataloging

In the past, serials and monographic cataloging in libraries have often taken different paths. Many libraries do not catalog serials at all. A large number of libraries have a separate serials catalog. Access points to serials records can be by main entry only, or by author, subject, and title.

Not until *AACR2* did the cataloging rules mandate treating serials "as much like other materials as possible. This is . . . achieved by accommodating all library materials in one common code, with one standard basis for description and one set of concepts for entry."[2] Because computer networks are now supplying cataloging data to libraries for serials and monographs, serials records are more complete—no longer as difficult or elusive for library users to find or public services librarians to interpret.

Public Services

The focal point for public services of serials is usually the current periodical room, with an adjacent serials information desk. Providing adequate service requires a commitment of high level and well-trained staff. Diane Stine writing about staffing has concluded that "little careful attention has yet been given to the nature of serials tasks and the type and level of staff most appropriate to perform them."[3]

Lack of training can be a problem. As recently as 1975, Benita Weber's survey of education for serials librarians enabled her to conclude that "serials librarians lack relevant library school education."[4] It can take years of on-the-job training for a librarian as well as a clerical to gain sophistication in dealing with serials. While that experience is being gained, it is possible that the collection could be dealt with inadequately or inappropriately.

It is interesting that the shelving arrangement of serials varies a great deal from library to library. If a library shelves its serials alphabetically, determining the shelf title can involve a choice between the popular name, the title as it is listed in indexes, the entry in the catalog, or the title as it appears on the piece itself. Further complicating this choice are title changes, and cataloging rules changes. If serials are shelved by call number, the reader must go to the catalog before going to the shelves. No matter which arrangement is chosen, there are problems for the library user.

Information about the amount of binding required for annual housekeeping of the collection can be useful in projecting future space needs. However, library predictors seem to confine themselves to the growth of the monograph collection as the leading indicator of library change.

Circulation procedures for libraries are built around circulation of the monograph. When a serial is circulated it is usually an exception to the rules. Because library use of serials often is not recorded, an important measure of library service is lost. Greater support for serials services could result if there were some standard measure of use, regularly compiled and widely reported.

Collection Maintenance

Inventory of serials is more difficult than inventory of monographs. It is easy to establish whether a monograph can be found, but a serials inventory can be an interminable process. For an effective inventory, staff must determine (1) which volumes and numbers have been published, (2) which of those are owned by the library, and then (3) whether the individual parts can be located. The publishing pattern, library record, and actual configuration of the pieces can be so complex that an experienced serials librarian is needed to verify accuracy of the record.

Monograph inventories in large libraries are rare, but serials inventories are almost unknown.[5] The amount of time needed to carry out an inventory is usually perceived as more costly than the benefits accrued. Most libraries prefer to believe their records are correct until proven wrong. It is then that an attempt to correct them ensues. Assigning responsibility for correcting existing serials records in a large library often falls between the cracks of the system. The serials cataloging staff is concerned with new materials, while the public services staff has many more pressing duties than the slow and unrewarding task of correcting minute records.

Theft and vandalism of serials is a major problem, caused in part by restrictive circulation policies. Library patrons often feel that they have "earned" the right to the material after going through the laborious process of finding it in the library.[6] Being denied the opportunity to take possession of it as a reward for their so-far successful behavior strikes them as unfair. As a consequence, pages are torn out or entire volumes stolen. The copy machine may have reduced the size of this problem to some extent. However, library users have no realization of the difficulty of replacing serials pages.

If a library goal is user convenience, one can argue against the practice of binding serials. The user wants one article, not the entire year's output. When copying an article, the binding is usually a handicap—its tight margins and general bulk making it difficult to get a good copy. Copying also breaks the binding and creates additional wear on the volume. Heavily copied serials might better be put into plastic binders for each individual issue. The long established practice of putting serials into bound volumes may have begun as an attempt to make the serial seem more like a monograph.

Bibliographic Accessibility

The traditional library card catalog was designed to provide bibliographic accessibility to the monograph collection. Cataloging practices provide access points to most of the information that users bring to the card catalog. Access to serials information is not so easily attained. Library users, to be successful, need to know which indexes to use and must acquire some skill in using them.

On-line data bases have done much to bring this mass of information under control. Information about the contents of serials, as well as union lists of serials titles, have been developing to the point where we now have an "information controllability explosion."[7] On-line data bases have filled an important gap in accessibility to information. A more recent development enables articles to be ordered on line, which further simplifies what has been a very time-consuming process.

THE IDEAL SERIALS LIBRARY

From this broad outline of the differences in library treatment of serials and monographs, we can begin to speculate on how libraries might be different if the special needs of serials were considered to be more important than those of monographs. They include:

1. More staff—A greater proportion of staff would be devoted to serials concerns, particularly acquisitions, claiming, and public service.
2. Better training—There would be more specialized education in library schools to train serials librarians.
3. Better measurement of service—The larger serials staff would now have the time and energy to collect statistics on serials use, which would influence library planning to a greater degree than at present.
4. Improved physical facilities—More serials collection growth information would be available to library planners, thereby assuring better serials accommodations in libraries.
5. Better awareness of library users' needs—Steps through which library users need to go to find serials in libraries would be simplified. This problem has been partially solved by databases, but there is still room for improvement.
6. Awareness of the serial as a physical entity—Some solution to the conflict between binding a serial and the wear and tear of the copying machine should be found.

An example of a library developed to handle serials lending is the British Lending Library at Boston Spa, Yorkshire. Because it is a closed-stack library conceived to handle a very large volume of demand, founders were free to develop a library with systems that are "simple, robust, and quick"[8] and to ignore many conventional library practices. The results are a collection that fills almost 3 million requests a year, and as many as 20,000 requests on a busy day. Titles are shelved alphabetically. The problem of location is handled by the "Keyword Index to Serial Titles (KIST)," which contains records of the 165,000 titles in the collection. Serials are no longer collected into bound volumes. Individual numbers are put into plastic binders color-coded by year, increasing their accessibility and ease of copying.

CONCLUSION

If libraries now treat serials like unruly monographs, imagine the change if serials were pre-eminent and monographs were treated like inconsequential serials. Assembling what we know about the difference in treatment of serials and monographs in our own libraries, we may come to the conclusion that treatment of the serial is inequitable and is based on outmoded ideas. Playing with the concept of a serials-centered library is a mental exercise that may result in an improved design.

Serials in libraries have assumed greater importance than ever before. Serials budgets consume a greater percentage of funds every year. Aids for cataloging and acquisition are achieving higher levels of sophistication. Bibliographic accessibility is at its peak. On-line order of serials can eliminate many steps in the research process, solving many problems of library listing, storage, and retrieval. It is up to librarians to discard outmoded practices in order to streamline library processes and improve patron accessibility.

REFERENCES

1. Osborn, Andrew D., *Serial Publications, Their Place and Treatment in Libraries.* 3d. ed. Chicago, American Library Association, 1980, p. 79.

2. Edgar, Neal, "Impact of AACR2 on Serials and Analysis," in *The Making of a Code: the Issues Underlying AACR2*, ed. Doris Hargrett Clack. Chicago: American Library Association, 1980, p. 92.

3. Stine, Diane, "Serials Department Staffing Patterns in Medium-Sized Libraries," *Serials Review*, 7 (July/September 1981): 83-87.

4. Weber, Benita M. "Education of Serials Librarians: A Survey," *Drexel Library Quarterly*, 11 (July 1975): 72-81.

5. Cook, Colleen, "Serials Inventory: a Case Study," *The Serials Librarian*, 5 (Winter 1980): 25-30.

6. Pinzelik, Barbara, "The Serials Maze: Providing Public Service for a Large Serials Collection," *Journal of Academic Librarianship*, 8 (May 1982): 89-94.

7. Koenig, Michael E. D., "The Information Controllability Explosion," *Library Journal*, 107 (November 1, 1982): 2052-2054.

8. "The British Library Lending Division, a Brief Guide," The British Library Lending Division, May 1983.

Half of a Conversation
With Neal Edgar

Jean Acker Wright

Appropriately, the topic of this contribution to a volume compiled to honor Neal was the subject of discussion and correspondence with him while he was compiling his work, *AACR2 and Serials: the American View.*[1] From 1973 until his death, we engaged in many hours of humor, debate, and sharing of ideas and concerns. To present these observations on the project which I described to him, without having an opportunity to get his reaction, seems strange. One of Neal's greatest contributions was to make people around him think and "brain-storm." Often, he served as a catalyst, stirring up activity by his influence.

In the introduction to his presentation, Neal quoted from my description of the development of Vanderbilt's "in-house" serials data base, and the manner in which reports received from catalogers reflect the types of activities related to maintenance of serials. I proposed the idea that librarians might be guilty of another "superimposition," and it would seem that the facts support that theory.

Since our data base includes titles cataloged prior to its origination in 1968, examples of various types of cataloging practices are included. This is typical of most serial records, union lists, and catalogs, and is one of the reasons that the adoption of new cataloging codes create such a "ripple effect" when they are added to an existing file. No matter how effective standards might be if consistently applied, even the conversion to the metric system for measurements has been strongly resisted because of the economic and cultural impact which will be the result. My purpose is not to comment on the merit of the rules, but on the effect that the changes make on the routine work in the library processing of serial publications.

Since January 1981, changes to the local data base have been coded to record the type of activity which caused the change. Although all of us who have worked with serials realize that when a serial is handled there is seldom only one change to be made, the coding represents the primary cause for revision of the record. For example, if a title ceases to be published, the receipt status changes, and recataloging to *AACR2* form and/or choice of entry might occur during the recataloging, but the transaction is coded as a cease of publication. The purpose was to discover what the actual impact of the major rules change was on the on-going work of serials staff. Librarians cannot control the actions of those who publish serials, and so must cope with the results. Technical services organizations exist to support the public service library functions of a library, and requests to move, cancel, or add materials to the collection form the basis for much of our activity. Serials work is in many ways reactive to the ''serial environment'' and to the institutional environment.

My premise is that a large portion of the changes were not related to *AACR2*, but that the timing of its adoption, as well as the abandoning of ''super-imposition'' was creating an amount of work which should have been better postponed until a larger number of libraries had abandoned manual files and could make global authority changes as well as being free of the requirements of making changes in a card catalog or catalogs to reflect changes in choice or form of entry.

The results of the survey are interesting, and may be typical of activities in other libraries, since our institution is a medium sized research library supporting programs in liberal arts, science and engineering, education, religion, music, and management. Although titles for the Medical and Law libraries are included, no coding was done for them. The list includes more than 27,000 serials, and of these, over 15,000 were added or changed in some way between January 1981 and mid-1984. Machine sorting the data base and other editorial changes account for many of these, and are irrelevant to the present discussion. Titles which have been deleted from the file are not included in the statistics.

July 22, 1984 the file included the following activity counts:

New titles	1,644
Title changes, current successive	479
Authority form change	692
AACR2 change	494
Other recataloging	1,103
Library required (change in receipt, etc.)	1,489

More than 3,030 new titles were added to the data base, from January through September 1983, so the extent of change to records is reflected by the fact that only 1,644 of them retain the code for a new title by mid-1984. A logical assumption is that most of the cataloging of these titles was *AACR2*, so that subsequent changes were caused by routine serial maintenance. Obviously, the successive entries caused by title changes account for a comparable number of recataloging activity for the earlier portions of the publications.

The most recent period for which complete figures are available is June through September 1984. During this time there were 726 change transactions. Meaningful totals are:

New titles	216
Titles newly added to data base	100
Title changes (new portion)	75
Title cessations (without successive title)	53
Title cessations (with successive title)	59
AACR2 changes	82
Other recataloging	62
Non-cataloging changes (receipt, fund, etc.)	69

Of the cataloging changes, 465 are caused by ''the nature of serials'' and 82 are the result of the change to *AACR2*. If my mathematics is correct, fifteen percent of the cataloging changes were necessitated by *AACR2*. This has some budgetary significance. As a matter of interest, five of the titles which were changed to *AACR2* form of entry during this period had previously been changed to reflect a change in the form of the authority under which they had been cataloged.

There is nothing definitive about these findings, but they may provide some source for comparison with other studies of the effects of change. I believe that Neal would enjoy considering the results, and others may want to imagine what his reaction might be.

REFERENCE

1. Edgar, Neal, ''AACR2 and Serials: the American View,'' *Cataloging and Classification Quarterly, 3* (1983): 2-3.

Analysis of Monographic Series

Ruth B. McBride

Most librarians and many library users are aware of the problems involved with serials and serials control. Much has been written on the difficulties libraries have with serials from their acquisition and cataloguing to binding and circulation, their title changes, erratic numbering, "spin-off" titles, etc. The same problems, plus some more, apply to "monographic series."

A monographic series is defined in the *Anglo-American Cataloguing Rules 2nd edition* as "a group of separate items related to one another by the fact that each item bears, in addition to its own title proper, a collective title applying to the group as a whole. The individual items may or may not be numbered."[1] Individual numbers may, of course, appear as monographs, as sub-sets, or worse yet, as sub-series. Some numbers may be issued without an author or authors and/or title, and may be identified only by the collective title. Some numbers may be issued in more than one series, each with its own numbering system. In some cases, two or more numbers may be issued in one physical volume. Monographic series are frequently issued as supplements to journals.

Monographic series are frequently very important research items, scholarly works which continue for many years, such as *Scrittori d'Italia*. All numbers of a series may be issued on a very narrow subject as with *Sage Annual Reviews of Drug and Alcohol Abuse* or *Developments in Petrology*. Alternatively, the topics covered by each number may be quite varied as with *Scripta Hierosolymitana* or *Colecao Documentos Brasileiros*. All sorts of publishers publish works in series: learned societies, governmental bodies, university presses, commercial publishers, conferences, etc. The *Memoirs of the American Mathematical Society,* the *Cooperative Groundwater Report (Illinois State Water Survey),* and *Studies in Consumer Credit* are examples of such publications. Indeed, monographic series are published in most disciplines. Important series appear, for example, in mathematics, agriculture, classics and education. Such

85

series as *Corpus Vasorum Antiquorum, Corpus Vitrearum Medii Aevi,* and the *Amsterdam Studies in the Theory and History of Linguistic Science* are well-known. This is a very common form of publication and one which has proliferated in recent years. It may be that publishers are aware of the penchant of librarians to order anything in a series with "standing orders" (often to avoid individual selection of a title). It may be that they simply recognize the desire of librarians to have a "complete run" of any series selected for the collection. Perhaps when publishers discover a "hot" topic with a known audience, they line up several authors expert in the subject, or at least a well-known editor, and start publishing a series. For them, it may mean a stable publication with identifiable readership and available authors. For authors, particularly academic researchers, such series may provide a ready vehicle for their work, as well as a continuing source of information in their subject area. It is probable that publishing in series is cost effective: standard format, regularly issued at specific intervals, mailing advantages, etc. Also, such series may be very useful to readers who, if they find one issue relevant, may find succeeding volumes equally so.

As individual issues of monographic series possess the qualities of both serials and monographs, librarians have had a choice in how to process them. Issues can be treated as either a number of a serial or as a monograph, or as a combination of the two. Series issued on a narrow subject, in successive parts, or intended to be read in sequence, may lend themselves to treatment as serials, that is, classed and catalogued together under the collective title. Each issue of a series with a weaker link between the individual volumes may more logically be treated as a separate monograph. When the decision is made to treat each volume as a separate monograph, the decision as to whether a series added entry is made for the collective title has been largely made by cataloguers. Different cataloguing codes offer different instructions, and the policies of the Library of Congress also varied through the years. Decker has noted the change of attitudes toward monographic series and series added entries, with the current cataloguing code, *AACR2*, making such entries practically mandatory.[2]

When the decision is made to treat a series as a serial, frequently a corollary decision is also made, whether "to analyze", that is, to provide an "analytical entry" for each individual volume. Such an entry was defined in the 1949 edition of *A.L.A. Cataloging Rules for*

Author and Title Entries as "the entry of some part of a work or of some article contained in a collection (volume of essays, serial, etc.).[3] The 1967 *Anglo-American Cataloging Rules* is somewhat more explicit, "an entry for a work or part of a work that is contained in a collection, series, issue of a serial, or other bibliographic unit for which another, comprehensive entry has been made. Analytical entries may be either separate, self-contained entries or added entries that are part of the cataloging of the larger work."[4] Analytical entry is defined in *AACR2* as simply "an entry for a part of an item for which a comprehensive entry has been made."[5]

Analysis of series has been an honest and sincere effort by librarians to give catalogue users the best of both worlds when it comes to monographic series. While the main series is classified and treated as a serial, each volume receives full descriptive cataloguing under author and/or title with subject headings, added entries, etc. They are shelved together for "browsers" who, if interested in one issue, may very well be interested in other issues of the series. A patron with a series citation can find the piece via the catalogue, as can the patron with an author/title citation for the individual volume. Of course, the item is also accessible through a search for the subject of either the series or the analyzed volume.

(While other kinds of analytics exist, e.g., "In" analytics for portions of a single volume as in a collection of essays or plays, only entries for monographs issued in series are being considered in this discussion.)[6]

All sizes and kinds of libraries have wrestled with the problems of cataloguing and processing of monographic series. Hyman describes the efforts of librarians to enhance the access to their growing collections through analysis from Panizzi and Ranganathan to Boolean searching of automated databases.[7] Mann notes that the "kind and size of the library must influence the cataloger in the number of analytical entries to be made."[8] She states a widespread theory that small, school, and special libraries may need to use analytical entries quite extensively in order to exploit the collection effectively, while in larger libraries, "analyticals will in most cases be limited to monographs contained in series and to important contributions in the transactions of learned societies."

While analysis has long been recognized as a valiant effort to serve the patron, there is evidence that libraries soon realized that the commitment was becoming more and more difficult to keep, with insufficient staff and growing backlogs. Flannery describes the

1949 efforts of Lehigh University Library to deal with the "deluge" of series and serials.[9] Noting that Lehigh had no consistent policy, "except that apparently an attempt had been made to analyze everything," the scarcity of cataloguers and overflowing card catalogue made it necessary to cease analyzing any routinely indexed series, or any appearing in standard bibliographies. Lehigh even went so far as to remove 50,000 analytical cards from the catalogue to alleviate the crowded conditions. The *Library of Congress Catalog of Printed Cards* was moved closer to the card catalogue for the use of patrons. "Important" series as well as other specific kinds of "individual items of special value" continued to receive analytic treatment.

Kilpatrick described similar efforts in 1950 to curtail the burgeoning responsibility of providing analytics at the University of Iowa Libraries.[10] Departmental librarians looked at each series being analyzed, investigated to see if and where it was being indexed, and, largely on that basis, made a decision whether to continue analysis. A note was made, where appropriate, that analysis had ceased, and information about indexes was added. However, Kilpatrick recognized some of the problems with this solution. He believed that while the sciences were comprehensively indexed, the humanities and arts were not. Also, many bibliographies, especially those of foreign language materials and literature, were inadequate, frequently omitting series information entirely. Since catalogue users rarely know the date of an item, considerable searching of indexes or/and bibliographies is necessary.

Whether material is indexed appears to be a frequent criteria in the decision to analyze. Mann recommends not analyzing those series which are routinely indexed, and Hyman traces the development of indexes as an alternative to analysis in considerable depth.[11,12]

In 1953, a panel of librarians, Beatrice M. Quartz, representing Wellesley College Library, Marian Harmon, University of Illinois Library, and Esther J. Piercy, Enoch Pratt Free Library, discussed "Policies for Analyzing Monographic Series," at the annual American Library Association conference.[13] The need for analysis was confirmed but the responsibility was growing so that ways to curtail it were explored. Indexes plus more selectivity were stressed by Quartz, as well as the need to depend upon the Library of Congress for cataloguing information. Harmon notes that while analysis is merely an effort to serve the patron, it is recognized that there is great economy for the Library in cataloguing a series as a serial and binding volumes together. Although patrons are accustomed to the practice, she raises the question of "how users of the catalog generally look for monographs published in series." Piercy reports the results of a survey of 20 large public libraries on the treatment of monographic series, which represent a relatively small part of a public library's cataloguing activity, and concludes that more information is needed to develop an intelligent policy regarding monographic series.

While some libraries appear to have developed a definite policy for the treatment of monographic series, some, like Lehigh, tried to analyze all of them. For some, the policy was simply to analyze those titles which the Library of Congress analyzed, that is, those titles for which LC cataloguing and cards were available. Any more comprehensive policy frequently involved decisions made by high-level professional librarians. As Harmon notes, it was not unusual for the head of cataloguing, the head of serials, a subject specialist, and/or the head of reference to meet in committee and look at every new series (in those cases of partial analysis, every volume) to determine the Library's treatment of it.[14] Which series should be catalogued as separates? Which series should be catalogued as serials? Which series should receive full analysis? Which partial analysis (only provide cataloguing for "important" volumes)? Which series should be catalogued as straight serials, without analysis? Which should receive author/title analytics only (the practice of not providing subject analysis or added entries, but to add author/title at the head of a unit card for the series, and the listing of each title in a "Contents" card behind the main entry card for the series). Or subject analysis only? What were the criteria by which series were judged to determine the library's treatment?

The criteria for such decisions were frequently an interesting mix of practicality and idealism. Availability of cataloguing staff and LC cataloguing in the form of analytical cards were primary considerations. The size of the pieces was important. If done as separates, each piece had to be bound separately; if done as a series, several volumes could be bound together. Was the series acquired by standing order or "purchased" as a serial, or did each new volume have to be selected and purchased separately? Did the series have a narrow subject area so that one classification would be suitable for all? Was it likely to be indexed in standard indexes? How was it likely to be cited? Did the departmental library for which it was destined have any preferences regarding analysis?

In 1952, the Library of Congress issued their criteria used to decide whether a series was to be catalogued as a series. These were as follows:

a. if an order of arrangement of the monographs in the series is indicated by the volumes in hand;
b. if the Library is likely to receive the issues of the series regularly;
c. if the monographs are closely related in subject content;
d. if the monographs are slight in format and would therefore best be kept together;
e. if the issues are consecutively paged.

Further, the series would be analyzed if some or all of the following factors existed:

a. if the monographs are of individual importance because of their authors, sponsoring bodies, subject interest, or for other reasons;
b. if the monographs have separate authors;
c. if the staff is qualified linguistically or by subject knowledge to undertake the task.[15]

By 1972, the Library of Congress was analyzing all analyzable series, except documents, technical reports, reprints from journals, and those requiring page analytics.[16]

The experience of the University of Illinois at Urbana over the past thirty years is probably typical of the experience of other academic institutions with regard to analyzed series. UIUC has analyzed over 15,000 series, with well over 250,000 analyzed volumes in its collection.

The 1952 policy regarding analyzed series was to analyze all monographic series for which LC cards were available except those series on a subject not within UIUC's primary collection areas. If LC cards were unavailable, series were analyzed only if the departmental library requested such treatment. Series indexed in standard indexes were not analyzed. If all issues of the series were likely to be on one subject, "author/title" analytics only were provided. This was the practice of listing all titles by author and/or title on a "Contents" card which was filed behind the main entry in the card catalogue, and later in the serial record. As volumes for new series were received, they were placed on a book truck by Acquisitions

Staff for review by a committee of experienced professional librarians. This committee met weekly to look at the materials on the "Decision Truck," as it was called, and to decide how each series should be catalogued, a difficult and time-consuming task.

The processing of analytics was the original "rapid" or "copy" cataloguing operation at UIUC. Many titles could be catalogued relatively cheaply and quickly with very little professional involvement. Once the decision was made to analyze a series, and the main series was catalogued with the proper call number assigned, clerical and student staff could "catalogue" the analytics by setting up "standing orders" for LC cards, searching the *National Union Catalog* for copy, or later using Title II cards, and constructing the call number by adding the volume number of the piece to the series call number. Cards were produced by the Card Division for each title and filed in the Main Catalogue with a "location" card. If cataloguing copy was not available, temporary cards with minimal information were filed into the catalogue and full cataloguing provided when it became available from LC. Individual titles were listed on "Contents" cards and filed behind the main entry. Pieces could be bound together as any other serial. However, each bibliographic unit was added to the holdings in the Serial Record, rather than the physical (circulatable) volume. Professional librarians catalogued the main series, supervised the operation, and did the necessary problem-solving. While backlogs were growing in other areas of cataloguing, backlogs were seldom seen in the Analytics Unit and the staff was proud of its fast turn-around time.

When technology appeared at UIUC in 1977, first in the form of OCLC, changes began to take place in the processes by which the Library treated its new materials. OCLC enabled the analytics staff to catalogue and process materials even faster and more efficiently. It eliminated the need for LC cards, including dependence on LC to analyze only those titles which LC analyzes. "Standing orders" for LC cards were cancelled. Any copy on OCLC could be revised for analytical use, and analyzed series became increasingly popular. More and more monographic series were sent for analysis.

Since analytics are circulated as volumes of serials, however, they were not added to the shelf list. Only the main series, as with serials, appeared in the shelf list. Consequently, with the next technological advance at UIUC, the development of LCS (Library Computer System), some problems became evident. Since LCS was developed as a simple circulation system by converting the shelf list to an automated database, the individual volumes of the series were included only as parts of the main series, and circulated only as a volume of the series. Thus, a patron with only the author and/or title of the individual volume will search LCS to no avail. A large and important segment of the collection is not clearly represented on the tool currently used for searching that collection. Patrons at UIUC, if persevering, can get help from Reference Librarians and other staff, and, after some experience, may recognize the problem themselves and be able to find the material in the card catalogue. Cards for analytics have been filed into the Supplement to the Card Catalogue, now frozen, with complete information. Patrons doing remote searches, however, unless they have a series entry, are less fortunate. It is still necessary to make the link with the main series or the call number, in order to search LCS for location and circulation information.

Some author/title information, for those titles for which full cataloguing (subject analysis, etc.) was considered unnecessary were added directly to the database, with a prefix added to the call number to alert patrons and staff that they were analytics, and, as such, must be circulated as a volume of a serial. Thus, some analytical titles are on LCS, and some are not, adding to the patrons' confusion.

These operational problems were recognized right away and possible solutions recommended. For one thing, LCS is meant to be an "interim" searching tool for circulation purposes only. Work has been going on for some time to develop an "online" catalogue. Full bibliographic records created through OCLC will be the basis of the online catalogue and will be interfaced with the present database. Thus all analytics catalogued since 1977 will appear in the online facility with an automatic link to the circulation record. Analytics catalogued prior to 1977 are still accessible in the card catalogue.

In the meantime OCLC has made it almost as easy and as cheap to catalogue an item as a separate as an analytic, so analysis of many series has been discontinued. Many items are being catalogued as separates with a series added entry. *AACR2*, used at UIUC since 1980, makes series added entry in most cases mandatory so it would appear that the patron is as well served by this approach.[17] The title appears on LCS immediately and circulation of the item as a monograph is straightforward.

While requiring a series added entry in most cases, *AACR2* has stipulated the form of that entry, frequently different from the forms of entry established by earlier cataloguing codes.[18] Straight serials, if catalogued according to an earlier code, are simply left alone, unless there is a title change, at UIUC. With analyzed series, earlier volumes will have the series traced one way (the main entry under which it is circulated) and later volumes will have the series traced another way with the only link being the call number. It is hoped that the capabilities of automation, with authority files and cross-references, can lead a patron through this bibliographic maze to locate the item he or she is seeking and provide him or her with the pertinent information.

But what about the catalogue user? Our attempts to provide the user with maximum information and a variety of access points have been fraught with inconsistency and lack of perceived logic through the years. Harmon's question of some thirty years ago remains unanswered. How does the patron access monographic series, and what treatment does he or she prefer? How is a monograph in series likely to be cited? By series? By individual author and/or title? How is the "browser" best served? By classing together? By classing separately? Does the subject involved make a difference? Is it more desirable to class together materials in the classics or in the sciences than in the humanities? Or do individual disciplines need individual treatment?

Most librarians agree that indexes and bibliographies are poor substitutes for a Library's analysis of monographs in series. Patrons are not generally sufficiently knowledgeable to do the kind of searching necessary, and excessive responsibility is placed on him or her to do so. Patrons may not look for monographic titles in indexes, which are generally thought of as guides to "periodical" literature. In many cases, the series information is not listed, and the patron might not recognize its significance if it were. Printed indexes are of uneven quality, become out-of-date quickly, and may not be sufficiently comprehensive. Even the present-day sophisticated online indexes are not a proper substitute for access through the Library's bibliographic tool, the catalogue, whatever its form, although subject searches through such services may well provide important bibliographic information. It is still necessary to search the Library's holdings to find the actual volume in question: does the Library own it? Is it available to the user?

Stenstrom and McBride, in a study of serial use by social science faculty, found that numbers of that group usually go to the Library for a specific article, having found a specific reference in footnotes or bibliographies.[19] Browsing accounted for very little of their use of the Library's serial collection. Yet Hyman concludes that browsing is an important part of library use for patrons of most American academic and research libraries, in spite of the fact that the value of such activity is difficult to demonstrate.[20]

Cochrane suggests that "use studies" done in the past with traditional card catalogues and printed indexes may not be valid with regard to online catalogues.[21] While users may have come to the library in search of a "known item" in the past, preliminary studies on the use of online catalogues seems to indicate a heavier use of subject searches. It is certainly logical that subject, keyword, and Boolean searches, easily performed online, would become popular search strategies for library users.

Cochrane further points out that professionals need to "understand the effects that online systems may have on traditional processes and services in libraries."[22] Moving from LC printed cards to computer terminals for cataloguing information, from card catalogues to online catalogues, and from printed indexes to bibliographic retrieval systems gives librarians an opportunity to revise traditional policies and enhance library service.

In processing monographic series using online cataloguing facilities, such as OCLC, it is no longer necessary to only "analyze if LC does." Numerous access points, including subjects, can be provided in an online catalogue. *AACR2* has standardized our approach to monographic series, requiring an added entry for most series. Librarians may now have the technological means to provide the best possible treatment of monographic series for library users. Certainly more information is needed with regard to how patrons approach certain monograph series. Then a logical, consistent yet flexible policy could be developed. It may be necessary for knowledgeable librarians to review each new series as it is received, as in the past, but they will be making their decisions according to different criteria, criteria based on an understanding of how series in the various disciplines should be treated.

There is no reason to believe that monographic series will cease to exist. They are an important and growing part of most collections and deserve first-rate treatment—as do readers of such series.

REFERENCES

1. *Anglo-American Cataloguing Rules,* 2nd ed. Chicago: American Library Association, 1978. p. 570.

2. Decker, Jean S., "AACR2 and Series," *Cataloging & Classification Quarterly,* 3 (Winter 1982/Spring 1983): 59-63.

3. *A.L.A. Cataloging Rules for Author and Title Entries.* Chicago: American Library Association, 1949. p. 229.

4. *Anglo-American Cataloging Rules. North American Text.* Chicago: American Library Association, 1967. p. 343.

5. *Anglo-American Cataloging Rules,* 2nd ed. p. 563.

6. *Ibid.,* p. 271.

7. Hyman, Richard J., *Analytical Access: History, Resources, Needs.* Queens College Studies in Librarianship, no. 2. Flushing, N.Y.: Queens College of the City University of New York, 1978.

8. Mann, Margaret, *Introduction to cataloging and the Classification of Books.* Second edition. Chicago: American Library Association, 1943. p. 153-54.

9. Flannery, Anne, "To Analyze or Not," *Journal of Cataloging and Classification,* 5 (Spring 1949): 42-43.

10. Kilpatrick, Norman L., "Serial Records in a University Library," *Journal of Cataloging and Classification,* 6 (Winter 1950): 33-35.

11. Mann, *Introduction to Cataloging,* p. 154.

12. Hyman, *Analytical Access.*

13. "Policies for Analyzing Monographic Series—a Panel Discussion," *Serial Slants,* 4 (July 1953): 124-40.

14. *Ibid.,* p. 133.

15. Library of Congress Processing Department. *Department Memorandum.* 77 (January 23, 1952).

16. Library of Congress Cataloging Service. *Bulletin.* 104. (May 1972).

17. *Anglo-American Cataloguing Rules,* 2nd ed. p. 324-25.

18. *Ibid.,* p. 40-41.

19. Stenstrom, Patricia and McBride, Ruth B., "Serial Use by Social Science Faculty: a Survey," *College & Research Libraries,* 40 (September 1979): 426-31.

20. Hyman, Richard J., *Shelf Access in Libraries.* ALA Studies in Librarianship, no. 9. Chicago: American Library Association, 1982. p. 115-20.

21. Cochrane, Pauline A., "A Paradigm Shift in Library Science," *Information Technology and Libraries,* 2 (March 1983): 3-4.

22. Cochrane, Pauline A., "Modern Subject Access in the Online Age," *American Libraries,* 15 (February 1984): 80-83.

The Challenge of Educating Library and Information Science Professionals: 1985 and Beyond

James E. Rush

"Nothing so needs reforming as other people's habits."

Mark Twain

INTRODUCTION

It is widely held that, in today's economy, information processing in all its aspects, accounts for well over half of the U.S. gross national product. Likewise, well over half of the labor force is engaged in service-oriented work which includes information processing. One must, of course, take care adequately to define "information processing," and to distinguish it from other services such as custodial, maintenance and repair, health care, burial, or entertainment.

Information processing generally involves the manipulation of data so as to reveal or highlight salient characteristics, features or properties of the data, or relationships among various data elements or classes of data elements. Information processing may yield a product (as a compilation, report, book), but the transformation of these "products" into quantities required for distribution and sale is a manufacturing process, not an information process. Information processing encompasses many professions and disciplines, including management, education, jurisprudence, accountancy, medicine (at least in respect to testing, diagnosis and record keeping), architecture, science and mathematics, advertising, and librarianship.

Unfortunately, librarianship has long been oriented strongly toward mere custodianship rather than toward active information processing. This posture of librarianship has given rise to

a. the creation and growth of information science as a separate discipline, and
b. the decline in stature of libraries (and librarians) of all types as evidenced by the economic realities of our times.

The current condition of librarianship, and to a lesser degree, information science, is the consequence of the academic programs which produce the bulk of the practitioners in these fields. As I will argue in more detail below, present academic programs in library and information science are largely barren and devoid of substance. The bulk of students who are attracted to these academic programs are ill-equipped to make their way in any other discipline.

In contrast with academic programs in other disciplines, where invention and innovation not only occur but are expected to occur, library and information science programs have rarely produced any significant inventions or innovations. Virtually every innovation which has (generally reluctantly) been adopted by libraries has come from people in other disciplines (chemistry being a notable example).

Academic programs in library and information science[1] have failed to keep pace with advances in technology and changes in society generally. This appears to be the result of

a. a failure to understand what librarianship is really all about;
b. the inbred nature of the profession, which has tended to be antagonistic to science and technology in particular, and to the commercial world in general;
c. the accreditation of academic programs by the profession itself, which forces programs to adhere to a norm of mediocrity;
d. the conception that the institution and its edifice are more important than vital user service, wherever or however such service may be rendered.

As a consequence, librarianship is at a cross-roads. The discipline has the opportunity to transform itself into a truly important, useful, and successful force in modern society. Failure to pursue this opportunity with intelligence and great vigor will result in the continued decline and failure of librarianship as a meaningful force in society.

Library Science vs. Information Science[2]

Within the last decade or so it has become fashionable to change the names of academic units offering education in librarianship to include the phrase "information science" or some similar phrase (such as "information management"). The problem is that this change of name, which reflects an attempt of librarians to expropriate "information science" as their own, has often been accompanied only by implementation of a single course in the curriculum, called (usually) information science. Such a change is thus essentially cosmetic in nature and cannot bring about the improvement of library science programs which is so sorely needed in today's information-oriented world. One cannot expect students in such academic programs to understand the nature and role of information processing and its importance to modern man.

The discipline generally called information science arose as a consequence of librarians' slowly but surely abdicating their role in organizing, summarizing, abstracting, indexing and in other ways providing effective access to materials contained in their libraries' collections. The growth of serial publications appears to have been the single greatest impetus for the formation of a cohesive field of study and practice variously called documentation, informatics, information service, or information science. Whereas libraries have been content to collect and house serial publications as though they were special cases of books, practitioners of information science have devoted much study and energy to the organization, classification, compilation, summarization and evaluation of data contained in serial publications, with the intent of reducing or eliminating the difficulty to which Lord Rayleigh referred when he wrote:

> By a fiction as remarkable as any to be found in law, what has once been published (no matter what the language) is usually spoken of as known, and it is often forgotten that the rediscovery in the library may be a more difficult and uncertain process than the first discovery in the laboratory.[3]

Thus the entire secondary information service enterprise has been developed within the scope of information science and outside the bounds of traditional librarianship.

So, too, have the tertiary information services, such as BRS, DIALOG, LEXIS, and the Source. In fact, the bulk of information retrieval systems, regardless of form or purpose, have been designed, developed and implemented outside of traditional librarianship. In some academic programs, all new information sources and systems have been referred to as "non-traditional," usually with the connotation that they are at best troublesome and of questionable acceptability. Today, librarians are "rediscovering" searching by keyword or phrase, using Boolean logical operators, relational operators, truncation, proximity, and other facets of information retrieval systems which were introduced in "non-traditional" systems beginning in the 1950s. The great upwelling of interest in on-line catalogs[4] clearly exemplifies the tardiness of librarians in adopting, let alone inventing, well-developed, proven technology to improve service to users.

Library science is not an empirical discipline, whereas information science is so considered. Librarianship is a practitioner's art, so that it is not surprising that virtually none of the theoretical or practical advances in the processing of information have arisen from research and development in academic departments of library science. It is also true that most of the technological advances which have been made in library operations[5] have been thrust upon librarians, rather than having been eagerly sought by them. Libraries even now insist upon "testing" systems such as OCLC or WLN to determine if the system will work in their organization, thereby disregarding the great mass of evidence all around them which demonstrates that the system does work. The reason for the "testing" is largely to determine if the system can be adopted without having to change existing library practices and procedures. At its logical extreme, this sort of attitude leads to rejection of a system because (to cite an example from personal experience) the system could not print subject headings in red ink, or print on the back of catalog cards. The librarian thus fails completely to realize that, by adopting the system, cards can be eliminated entirely. Moreover, present technology will permit data to be displayed in multiple colors, intensities and contrasts, for emphasis or ease of recognition by users. No printed catalog can match the capabilities of video display technology for data presentation.

Library science is tradition-bound, static, and isolated from the world of the user. That is why one sees so few librarians in a library. They tend mostly to be in the "back room," comfortable in the safety of the known, the common, the ordinary. Those who call themselves information scientists (specialists, or what have you) have no more courage or intelligence than do librarians. But they are not crushed by tradition, and they have learned that their true role is service to the user. They recognize the dynamic nature of the information business (yes, it is a business), and there is some understanding among them of how little we know of information processing and communication. Information science has tended to exhibit a spirit of exploration and discovery, while librarianship has tended to be defensive, protective of tradition, and suspicious of invention and innovation. Librarianship has tended to be antagonistic to the commercial world, whereas information science has made a strong alliance with business. Information science has shown a willingness to scrap ideas which will not stand up to practical tests and to abandon products and processes which have outlived their usefulness. Librarianship, on the other hand, has shown a remarkable interest in preserving the status quo and, in the words of Markuson (in reference to cataloging), in "working their exquisite local petit point, having refined bibliographic embroidery to a high art form."[6]

Both librarianship and information science are, at the heart, concerned with communication and thus belong together as a single field of study and endeavor. The amalgamation of these two fragments of the same discipline must begin with our educational institutions. Moreover, the amalgamation cannot be evolutionary (the time is past for that), it must be revolutionary. Otherwise, there will likely remain no vital educational programs to serve as the crucible for the process.

Library and Information Science Programs

The vitality of many library and information science programs is on the decline or has been snuffed out altogether. This is astonishing when the growth of the information industry is accelerating and when our understanding of information processing is still in its infancy.

One of the oldest and most respected schools, the Baxter School of Information and Library Science, has, for a variety of reasons, been terminated by Case Western Reserve University. It is reported that the School of Library and Information Management at the University of Southern California will be closed as well. The program at Ball State University is being down-graded to the undergraduate level. Many other programs have experienced decreased enrollment, reduced budgets, and loss of faculty. The reason for the failure of library and information science programs, as well as for the weakness of many others, stems from a perception on the part of parent-institution administrations, potential students, prospective employers, and funding sources that existing programs are irrelevant to the needs of the institution and the information industry today. Library and information science academic programs have failed to maintain accurate models of the work-a-day world and the importance of information processing, in its broadest sense, in that world. Administrators and faculty of these programs have therefore failed to develop and enhance curricula designed to produce graduates with the relevant knowledge, skills and intellectual acuity to meet the challenge of today's and tomorrow's information-oriented, global society.

Inspection of typical course offerings comprising a library and information science curriculum reveals

a. that courses deal with media, but not with messages;
b. that courses deal with sources but not their content;
c. that courses deal with age groups rather than with the diverse spectrum of information users regardless of age (including handicapped, disadvantaged, suburbia vs. inner city, public officials, private business people, and entrepreneurs);
d. that courses deal with historical rather than modern techniques and technology.

Thus one finds courses in the history of the book and printing, but rarely a course on modern methods of printing and production of printed materials (bookform or not). Courses on the history of the library are offered, but not courses which address the role of the library as the community information service. Courses deal with the administration of specific types of libraries, but rarely is a course offered or recommended which deals with modern management (as opposed to administration). What programs are there which offer or require as part of the curriculum courses in

— marketing and sales
— information services to business and industry
— budgeting and finance
— planning
— telecommunication
— electronic publishing
— records management
— regional network services and operation

— information brokerage
— indexing
— abstracting
— computational linguistics
— theory of information and communication
— information system operation
— personnel management
— measurement of the effectiveness of services
— revenue generation
— delivery of information services and products
— basic political science
— sociology
— computer architecture
— introduction to formal linguistics
— computer programming
— information processing in the year 2000 and beyond
— information services in space
— litigation support
— effective space utilization
— mathematics and statistics
— organization and governance
— cost analysis and accounting
— economics
— the free enterprise system
— data base management
— graphics
— information retrieval (theory and techniques)
— writing
— vocabulary management and control?

This list is by no means comprehensive, but it clearly suggests the nature and scope of modern information and library science. To be sure, some existing courses should be retained (but strengthened and updated), including cataloging (with emphasis on serials and other non-book materials), classification (principles, purposes, practice), circulation management and control (including interlibrary loan), collection development and management, acquisition of materials and services, reference services (strong emphasis), and public access to the information resources of the library or of its peer organizations. All courses should emphasize the similarities among all facets of the information industry, rather than insisting on dwelling on the differences. Different types of libraries there may be, but their similarities far outweigh any differences among them.

Students of library and information science must learn that a library, like any other enterprise, has a market to establish and serve, has a range of products and services to sell[7] to this market, and must show (in one way or another) a positive return on investment or, ultimately, go out of business. Librarians, particularly academicians, must learn that academic programs of library and information science have quite similar characteristics (e.g., markets, products and services, financial viability) and can only prosper and grow when close attention is paid to profitable performance.

For academic units of library and information science, there is a broad and growing market for people with requisite knowledge and skills in information processing. No longer are traditional libraries the sole market. Every conceivable business, government, sectarian entity, or educational institution has significant requirements for personnel who have knowledge and skills in information processing. It is the responsibility of library and information science programs (as it is for all other types of academic programs) to insure that they produce graduates who are employable within their chosen discipline, and to insure that production of graduates corresponds with demand both in number and in kind. Everything else an academic unit does must be based upon this fundamental concept.

Existing programs in library and information science seem not to embody this concept. Nor do existing programs seem to recognize or have a relation to a well-organized, comprehensive curriculum. A review of the library and information science programs listed and described in the *American Library Directory* (1984)[8] indicates that there are some 300 programs throughout the United States. Nevertheless, there are only 74 (25%) which seem to offer fairly comprehensive programs, and almost none of these address the sorts of topics listed on pages 102 and 103. Table 1 presents a summary of the library and information science programs reported in the *ALD*. These programs present a confused and incoherent picture of basic academic requirements at either the undergraduate or graduate levels of education. About one-third of the programs are concerned with media and many of these are part of a department, college or school of education. Another third of the programs deal in the main with library technician training and most of these programs amount to undergraduate minors rather than full-fledged degree programs in their own right. A few of the programs lead to baccalaureate de-

Table 1.   Summary of library and information science academic units (schools, departments, etc.) in the
United States (from American Library Directory),
1984.

STATE	MEDIA	TECHN.	LIB/INFO	OTHER	TOTAL	ACCRED
		----------PROGRAMS----------				
Alabama	5	1	2	-	8	1
Arizona	-	1	3	-	4	1
Arkansas	4	-	2	-	6	0
California	6	6	5	2	19	4
Colorado	2	1	1	-	4	1
Connecticut	-	1	1	-	2	1
DC	1	1	1	-	3	1
Florida	4	-	2	-	6	2
Georgia	7	1	3	-	11	2
Hawaii	-	-	1	-	1	1
Idaho	2	1	-	-	3	0
Illinois	10	6	4	1	21	4
Indiana	3	1	3	-	7	2
Iowa	1	3	1	-	5	1
Kansas	4	-	1	-	5	0
Kentucky	3	-	3	-	6	1
Louisiana	-	11	1	-	12	1
Maine	-	1	-	-	1	0
Maryland	1	1	1	-	3	1
Massachusetts	2	2	1	2	7	1
Michigan	1	3	3	-	7	2
Minnesota	1	3	1	-	5	0
Mississippi	-	2	1	1	4	1
Missouri	1	6	1	1	9	1
Montana	2	-	-	1	3	0
Nebraska	3	-	-	1	4	0
Nevada	-	1	-	-	1	0
New Jersey	3	1	1	2	7	1
New Mexico	1	1	-	1	3	0
New York	-	1	8	-	9	8
North Carolina	3	3	4	1	11	3
North Dakota	3	1	-	-	4	0
Ohio	5	3	2	1	11	2
Oklahoma	3	1	1	1	6	1
Oregon	1	-	-	2	3	0
Pennsylvania	-	7	3	4	14	3
Rhode Island	-	-	1	-	1	1
South Carolina	2	-	1	-	3	1
South Dakota	2	2	-	-	4	0
Tennessee	-	6	2	1	9	2
Texas	3	3	3	1	10	3
Utah	3	-	1	-	4	1
Virginia	3	2	-	-	5	0
Washington	1	1	1	2	5	1
West Virginia	1	5	-	1	7	0
Wisconsin	-	7	3	1	11	2
Wyoming	1	-	-	-	1	0
Puerto Rico	-	-	1	-	1	0
TOTALS	98	97	74	27	296	58
% of Total	33	33	25	9	100	20

grees whose nature cannot be easily categorized. Only about 25% of the programs are broad spectrum library and information science programs, and most of these do not go much beyond the bounds of traditional librarianship. Only about 20% (58) of the programs are accredited by the American Library Association, and all of these are included among the 74 library and information science programs. The table includes those programs which have been or soon will be terminated or down-graded.

Figure 1 is a bar chart showing the relative proportion of library and information science programs which have been founded in each five-year interval from 1890. Over half of the programs have been inaugurated since 1960 (some 30% since 1970), although only 32% of accredited programs were formed after 1960 (6% after 1970). This data indicates that while many of the programs have had a relatively fresh start, they have not taken the opportunity to modernize curricula, perhaps in part because of the accreditation process.

Accreditation and Tenure

These are the twin foes of enlightened, vital, dynamic and successful academic programs, despite the fact that they were not intended to be.

Accreditation in and of itself is not a bad thing. The purpose of accreditation programs is to provide a mechanism to insure that academic programs meet or exceed standards established by the profession of which the accreditation program is a part. The problem is that in actual practice the success of an accreditation program (as measured both by the members of the profession and by the world at large) depends upon emphasis on state-of-the-art standards rather than on tradition, upon objectivity rather than subjective judgement, upon honesty rather than political expediency, and upon a clear notion of reality rather than upon the norm of myth. Accreditation by its very nature is highly politically charged, is performed by people who are often unfamiliar with the current trends in the industry or with research in the field, and in any case is conducted so as to maintain the mystique of the profession (at least until the profession lapses into a coma).

If accreditation is to achieve its real purpose, it must be based upon a clear conception of the nature, status, and likely future of the discipline it governs. It must be clear about the economic reality of

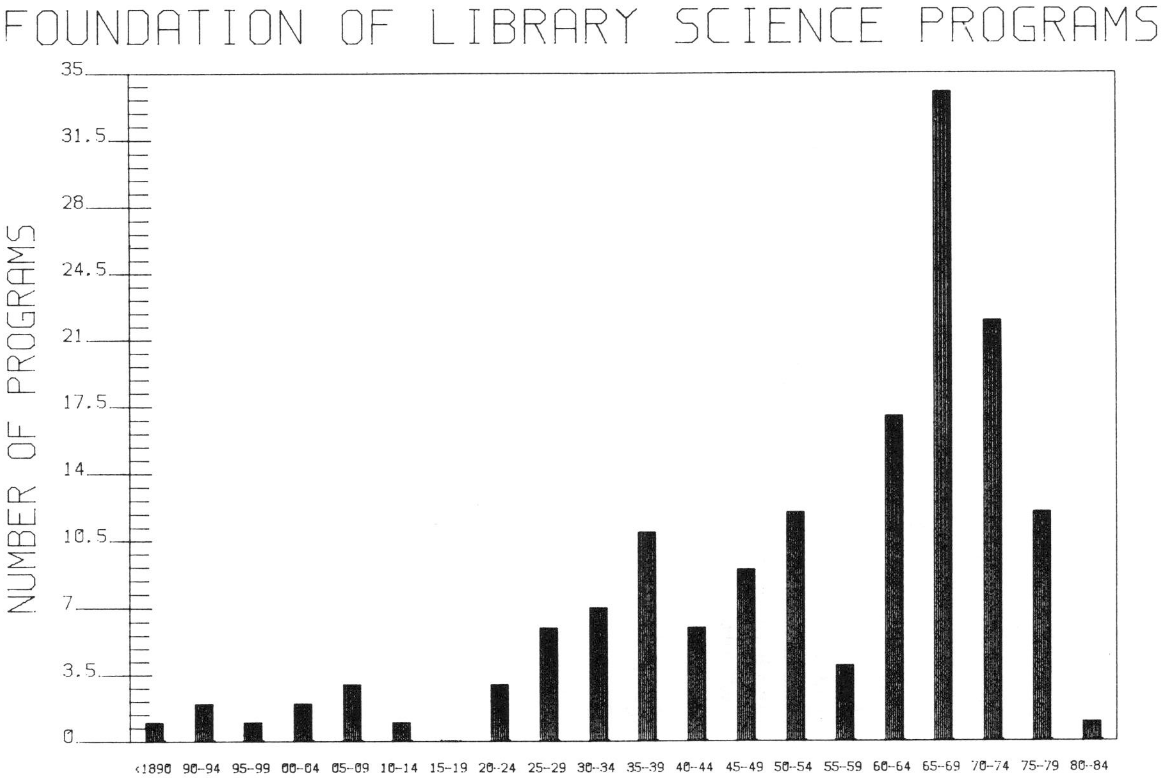

FIGURE 1. Bar chart showing population of library programs vs. year of foundation.

the industry in which members of the discipline practice, and it must facilitate rather than frustrate growth, adaptation and change.

Accreditation programs must be reviewed and revised frequently in fields as dynamic as information processing. The ALA *Standards for Accreditation, 1972*[9] were revised in 1977. Several minor revisions have since been made. In spite of these revisions, the standards do not adequately address the required content of academic programs for effective education of students to enable them to obtain and perform successfully in jobs in the information industry. The accreditation program seems to assume that the discipline is well-defined and that process is more important than product. Unfortunately neither of these is true. What is needed is a set of standards for a modern curriculum and for maintenance of the curriculum current with changing times. Such standards cannot be achieved until the present and future nature of the profession is recognized.

Tenure, which was meant to protect the faculty from summary dismissal, has become a bastion of defense for the incompetent. All too often, faculty who have acquired tenure (earned is too strong a word), soon retire on the job, and no longer show interest in new ideas, thought or directions (certainly none which would place their jobs in jeopardy). They therefore should be dismissed for malpractice, a concept which seems not to apply in education.

Tenure is wrong because it is granted for life, because it is granted by "senior" faculty (the old guard), and because it is used as an excuse for dismissing young, dynamic, but less experienced faculty either because of budget crunches, failure to publish the necessary quantity of verbiage (irrespective of its quality), or because they espouse ideas which do not accord with the cherished beliefs of the tenured faculty. Tenure often fails to recognize teaching ability and/or administrative ability, both of which are essential qualities in academic faculty. Library and information science can ill afford to turn away bright young faculty simply because there are no tenured positions available, or because older faculty denied them tenure for selfish reasons. The faculty one would truly want are those who do not need tenure. Those who need tenure are often those one should not have as members of a faculty. What is needed instead are standards of performance against which faculty can be measured at least annually if not more frequently. In this way academic faculty will more likely remain active and intellectually alive throughout their careers.

One final observation on academic faculty: no person should be hired to an academic faculty who was trained by that faculty, and no person should be hired to an academic faculty who has not had at least five year's experience in the industry the faculty serves. In this way, inbreeding will be minimized, and the exchange of ideas between the academic institution and the information industry will be increased. Most importantly, students will benefit from new ideas and the practical experience of the faculty.

Library and Information Science Degrees

Library and information science is too broad and complex a field to allow the present degree programs at most academic institutions to remain unaltered. In the first place, it is necessary that every legitimate library and information science program begin at the undergraduate level. The baccalaureate degree should be designed not only to produce graduates who can work effectively in libraries and information centers (however defined), but who have the basic training to continue toward a graduate degree. The present one-year master's programs are quite inadequate to legitimately be called graduate degrees, much less degrees which qualify a person as a member of the profession.

Since information processing transcends traditional subject disciplines, the undergraduate program should be designed as an interdisciplinary program, with specific degree programs focused on business, medicine, science and mathematics, law, agriculture and home economics, art, and so on. These programs could be administered jointly by the library and information science unit (department) and by the department, school or college which is concerned with the specific subject orientation. In any case, their content, and the expected competence of the graduate must be established and maintained by both academic units.

In addition, the library and information science unit should have a specific degree program designed for direct admission to the graduate program. In this case, a minor or minors in other subject disciplines would be required. This version of the undergraduate program should focus on developing practitioners in the field of information processing itself, including workers in networks, consortia, bibliographic services (OCLC, BRS), and other segments of the information industry.

Emphasis in the undergraduate degree program should be on quantitative skills, and on knowledge and skills which will serve the graduate well in actual work settings. There is no escaping the fact that computing in all of its facets is an essential part of information processing and that students in library and information science programs must not only be familiar with computing, but be skilled in its application in information processing as well.

The master's program must no longer be an undergraduate program in disguise. The master's program should be a two-year program which emphasizes advanced course work *and* research. It is essential that graduates at the master's level not only assimilate existing knowledge and skills more advanced than those obtained at the undergraduate level, but also make a real contribution to the body of knowledge which comprises the field. By research, I do not mean the sort which amounts to little more than the assembly of a series of quotations from the published literature. What I mean is research of a concrete, quantitative nature which in some modest way (at least) advances our understanding of information processing or which contributes new techniques to the arsenal. The very foundation of information science is the ability to properly frame questions for which answers are sought. That is what research is all about, and that is why research must be a significant part of the master's program.

The doctoral program should focus almost entirely on research. A student's research program must be designed to lead to a significant contribution to our understanding of information processing either in theory or in practice. The doctoral program (and any post-doctoral programs which might be implemented) must serve as the source of invention and innovation within the information processing field. It will be inadequate for doctoral dissertations to deal with material already in the literature, except as the foundation of the research which the candidate performs. Here, as at lower degree levels, interdisciplinary programs are desirable, although they will prove troublesome to most academicians. Graduates should be prepared for significant roles throughout the information industry, and ultimately for roles in academia.

It is essential that laboratory work form a significant part of the curriculum. This means that adequate complements of equipment, facilities and services must be provided by the academic unit. Laboratory exercises and experiments must be an integral part of the courses which comprise the curriculum, not simply afterthoughts, as seems to be the case today.

All three degree levels would benefit from inclusion of requirements for practical experience in actual work settings. The first resource would be the library system of the parent institution. It would be highly desirable that the library be a teaching library, rather than a reluctant partner in the educational process. In addition, opportunities for experience in industry, regional network offices, on-line service organizations, and other facets of the information industry should be developed and made requirements of degree programs.

Finally, students of library and information science must be taught that they are training for careers in a business of great importance, and that a high degree of competence and confidence are essential accomplishments. The only way present perceptions and attitudes of the general public toward library and information science practitioners can be improved is to produce graduates with the knowledge, skills and attitude that people respect and admire. Success breeds success.

Beyond degree programs, there is a strong need for continuing education on the part of everyone who works in the information industry. In fact, it should be required that people who wish to retain their professional standing pursue continuing education on a regular basis. Both educational institutions and employers can aid in providing opportunities for continuing education, and present members of the profession should work hard to see that these opportunities are realized. There is also room for commercial firms to offer continuing education, as is the case in other disciplines. No one who earns a degree in library and information science can honestly claim to be a professional unless he or she continuously maintains an awareness and knowledge of the subject matter with which he or she must deal on a routine basis. This knowledge and awareness can only be achieved through reading, seminars, workshops, and formal course work.

CONCLUSION

It remains to be seen if librarians can meet the challenge of properly educating students of library and information science. There is little time left in which to develop the necessary programs and to overhaul the profession. What I have proposed here is a radical departure from most of the existing academic programs. My proposal, like the King Research "New Directions" report[10] will no doubt be debated or ignored rather than taken as the basis for immediate action. That is the way librarianship responds to new ideas. Nevertheless, I am convinced that only radical action can save librarianship as a viable profession.

REFERENCES

1. Keep in mind that the phrase "information science" (and its variants, such as information management) has been added to the title of library science programs fairly recently, and that very little change in the programs themselves has occurred.

2. The use of the word "science" in either of these phrases is, at best, only weakly applicable, but information science has a stronger claim to the use of the word than does library science at present.

3. Lord Rayleigh. Quoted in: Mellon, M. G. *Chemical Publications: Their Nature and Use.* New York, NY: McGraw-Hill, 1965, p. 17.

4. Often called on-line public access catalogs, as though there were an on-line private access catalog as an alternative.

5. Which almost exclusively address ways of doing traditional library work faster and/ or more efficiently.

6. Markuson, B. E. "Cooperation and Library Network Development," *College and Research Libraries,* 40 (1979), 125.

7. The myth that library services are free must be dispelled. Library services are quite costly, and the evidence to support the conjecture that the cost is justified by the benefits is lacking. I do not suggest that everyone who uses the services and resources of a library should be required to pay in proportion to the benefit received, but it is clear that those who do pay for library services are demanding more than they perceive they obtain in benefits. Librarians must understand what every business person knows implicitly, namely that every product or service must have an identifiable market, must be offered at a price which is acceptable to the market, and must realize a profit. Otherwise, the enterprise fails.

8. Jaques Cattell Press (Ed.). *American Library Directory,* 37th Edition (2 Vols.). New York, NY: R. R. Bowker Company, 1984, 2109 pp.

9. Committee on Accreditation. *Standards for Accreditation, 1972.* Chicago, IL: American Library Association, 1973.

10. Griffiths, J.-M., et al. *New Directions in Library and Information Science Education.* [A report prepared for the U.S. Department of Education] Rockville, MD: King Research, 1985.

"Give Peace A Chance":
Subject Access to Material
on Nukes, Militarism, and War

Sanford Berman

The issues of nuclear power, arms control, and defense demand serious attention. To make intelligent decisions, citizens must be well-informed. Most libraries have recognized that need by stocking a variety of relevant material. But those same libraries, if they unthinkingly accept LC "copy" and subject headings, may actually restrict access to the very items they have painstakingly secured, for material that can't be readily identified through the catalog is likely to be unfound and unused, thus contributing little to the democratic process. To illustrate, here's a comparison between Hennepin County Library and Library of Congress "nuke" and peace forms:

+HCL	+LC
ARMS SALES	None.
ATOMIC VETERANS	None.
CHILDREN AND NUCLEAR WARFARE	None.
CHRISTIAN PEACE MOVEMENT	None.
DRAFT	MILITARY SERVICE, COMPULSORY
DRAFT COUNSELING	None.
DRAFT PROTESTS	None.
DRAFT REGISTRATION	None.
DRAFT RESISTANCE	MILITARY SERVICE, COMPULSORY—DRAFT RESISTERS
FALLOUT SHELTERS	ATOMIC BOMB SHELTERS
FIRST STRIKE (MILITARY STRATEGY)	None.

+HCL	+LC
HIBAKUSHA [i.e., Japanese A-bomb survivors]	None.
HIROSHIMA—ATOMIC BOMBING, 1945	HIROSHIMA SHI (JAPAN)— BOMBARDMENT, 1945
LIMITED NUCLEAR WAR	None.
MILITARY-INDUSTRIAL COMPLEX	None.
MISSILES	BALLISTIC MISSILES; GUIDED MISSILES
NUCLEAR DISARMAMENT	ATOMIC WEAPONS AND DISARMAMENT
NUCLEAR DETERRENCE STRATEGY	None.
NUCLEAR FREEZE CAMPAIGN	None.
NUCLEAR HOLOCAUST	None.
NUCLEAR POWER	ATOMIC ENERGY; ATOMIC POWER
NUCLEAR POWER POLICY	ATOMIC ENERGY POLICY
NUCLEAR POWER REGULATION	None.
NUCLEAR TERRORISM	None.
NUCLEAR WARFARE	ATOMIC WARFARE
NUCLEAR WEAPONS POLICY	None.
NUCLEAR WINTER	None.
PEACE CONVERSION	None.
PEACE MOVEMENT	None.
SURVIVAL (AFTER NUCLEAR WARFARE)	None.
UNILATERAL NUCLEAR DISARMAMENT	None.
WAR TAX RESISTANCE	None.

And these are tracing-contrasts between HCL- and LC-cataloged titles:

Adams, Ruth.
       The final epidemic: physicians and scientists on nuclear war. 1981.

PARTIAL CONTENTS: Economics of the arms race. -Nuclear weapons: characteristics and capabilities. -Consequences of radioactive fallout. -Occurrence of cancer in atomic bomb survivors. -Burn casualties. -Preventing nuclear war. -International Physicians for the Prevention of Nuclear War.

LC: No record found.

HCL: 1. International Physicians for the Prevention of Nuclear War.
      2. Nuclear warfare—Medical aspects.
      3. Arms race—Economic aspects.
      4. Nuclear weapons.
      5. Radioactive fallout—Health hazards.
      6. Nuclear power and cancer.

Albert, Michael.
Beyond survival: new directions for the disarmament movement. 1983.

PARTIAL CONTENTS: Feminism and militarism. -Racism: fuel for the war machine. -Labor and disarmament: the meeting of social movements.

LC: No record found.

HCL: 1. Nuclear disarmament.
      2. Peace movement—United States.
      3. Feminism and militarism.
      4. Racism and militarism.
      5. Labor unions and disarmament.

Alexander, Sidney.
Peace research and activists groups: a North American directory. 1982.

LC: No record found.

HCL: 1. Peace movement—United States—Directories.
      2. Peace—Information services.
      3. Peace research—Directories.

Barnaby, Frank.
The nuclear arms race: control or catastrophe? 1982.

PARTIAL CONTENTS: Effective deterrence. -The physical and medical effects of nuclear weapons. -Averting holocaust? Strategies of popular intervention and initiative in the Thermonuclear Age. -The scientists' responsibility.

LC: 1. Atomic warfare—Congresses.
     2. Deterrence (Strategy)—Congresses.
     3. Strategic forces—Congresses.
     4. Atomic weapons and disarmament—Congresses.

HCL: 1. Nuclear disarmament.
     2. Deterrence (Military strategy).
     3. Nuclear warfare—Moral and ethical aspects.
     4. Nuclear warfare—Medical aspects.
     5. Antinuclear movement.
     6. Scientists—Social responsibility.
     7. Arms race.

Bergel, Peter.
The whole freeze catalog. 1982.

LC: No record found.

HCL: 1. Antinuclear movement—Directories.
     2. Nuclear disarmament—Bibliography.
     3. Nuclear disarmament—Information services.
     4. Nuclear freeze campaign—Information services.
     5. Nuclear freeze campaign—Mediagraphy.
     6. Nuclear freeze campaign—Directories.

Berger, Jason.
The military draft. 1981.

PARTIAL CONTENTS: The all-volunteer army. -The question of registration. -For a military draft. -Against a military draft. -The women's issue.

LC: 1. Military service, Compulsory—United States—Addresses, essays, lectures.
     2. Military service, Voluntary—United States—Addresses, essays, lectures.

HCL: 1. Draft.
2. Volunteer army.
3. Women and the draft.
4. Draft registration.

Briggs, Raymond.
When the wind blows. 1982.

LC: 1. Atomic warfare—Popular works.

HCL: 1. Survival (after nuclear warfare)—Comic
books, strips, etc.
2. Civil defense—Comic books, strips, etc.
3. Fallout shelters—Comic books, strips, etc.
4. Nuclear weapons policy—Comic books,
strips, etc.
5. Gullibility—Comic books, strips, etc.

Caldicott, Helen.
Nuclear madness: what you can do! 1978.

PARTIAL CONTENTS: Radiation. -The cycle of death.
-Nuclear sewage. -Plutonium. -M.A.D.

LC: 1. Atomic power.

HCL: 1. Antinuclear movement.
2. Nuclear weapons.
3. Nuclear power and cancer.
4. Radiation—Health hazards.
5. Radioactive pollution.

Clark, Ian.
Limited nuclear war. 1982.

LC: 1. Atomic warfare.
2. Limited war.

HCL: 1. Limited nuclear war.

Cohen, Sam.
The truth about the neutron bomb: the inventor of the
bomb speaks out. 1983.

LC: 1. Neutron bomb.

    2. Atomic warfare—Moral and ethical aspects.
    3. United States—Military policy.

HCL: 1. Neutron bomb.
     2. Nuclear warfare—Moral and ethical aspects.
     3. Nuclear weapons policy.

Collins, Larry.
The fifth horseman; a novel. 1980.

LC: No subject tracings.

HCL: 1. Nuclear terrorism—Fiction.
     2. International intrigue—Fiction.

Federation of American Scientists.
Seeds of promise: the first real hearings on the nuclear arms freeze. 1983.

Includes "A call to halt the nuclear arms race."

LC: 1. Atomic weapons and disarmament—
      Congresses.

HCL: 1. Nuclear freeze campaign.
     2. Arms race.

Ford, Daniel F.
Beyond the freeze: the road to nuclear sanity. 1982.

LC: 1. Arms control.
     2. Atomic weapons and disarmament.

HCL: 1. Nuclear disarmament.

Ford, Daniel F.
The cult of the atom: the secret papers of the Atomic Energy Commission. 1982.

LC: 1. Atomic power—United States.
     2. United States. Atomic Energy Commission.

HCL: 1. Nuclear power regulation.
     2. Nuclear power plants—Safety measures.
     3. Nuclear power industries—History.
     4. Government accountability—Case studies.
     5. Corporate accountability—Case studies.

Freeman, Leslie J.
Nuclear witnesses: insiders speak out. 1981.

Includes a chronology of events in the history of nuclear power and interviews with medical researchers, nuclear power workers, uranium miners, widows of uranium miners, a Navajo organizer, and an atomic bomb test veteran.

LC: 1. Atomic energy industries—United States.
     2. Atomic workers—Diseases and hygiene—
        United States.
     3. Atomic workers—United States—Interviews.

HCL: 1. Nuclear power—History.
     2. Nuclear power industries—Personal narratives.
     3. Nuclear power industry workers—Interviews.
     4. Atomic veterans—Interviews.
     5. Whistle blowing—Personal narratives.
     6. Nuclear power—Health hazards—Personal
        narratives.
     7. Plutonium—Health hazards—Personal
        narratives.

Governance of nuclear power. 1981.

LC: 1. Atomic energy policy—United States.
     2. Atomic power-plants—Safety measures—
        Government policy—United States.

HCL: 1. Nuclear power regulation.

Gyorgy, Anna.
No nukes: everyone's guide to nuclear power. 1979.

PARTIAL CONTENTS: Health dangers. -Safety along the fuel cycle. -Dictionary of nuclear terms. -Some alternatives. Conservation. Recycling. Going solar. -Development of a movement.

LC: 1. Atomic power.
     2. Atomic power-plants.
     3. Atomic power industry.
     4. Power resources.

HCL: 1. Nuclear power.
     2. Antinuclear movement.

3. Nuclear power industries.
4. Nuclear power—Dictionaries.
5. Alternative energy sources.

Hedemann, Ed.
Guide to war tax resistance. 1983.

PARTIAL CONTENTS: The IRS audit and appeals process. -Alternative funds. -Personal histories. -Legal tax objection. -World Peace Tax Fund. -WTR groups & counselors.-Military spending throughout United States history.

LC: 1. Tax evasion—United States.
      2. Pacifists—United States.

HCL: 1. United States. Internal Revenue Service.
      2. War tax resistance.
      3. War tax resistance groups—Directories.
      4. World Peace Tax Fund.
      5. Military expenditures—United States.

Johnson, R. Charles.
Don't sit in the draft. 1980.

LC: No record found.

HCL: 1. United States. Selective System.
      2. Draft resistance.
      3. Conscientious objectors.

Jungk, Robert.
The new tyranny: how nuclear power enslaves us. 1979.

PARTIAL CONTENTS: Radiation fodder. -Atomic terrorists. -Organizations.

LC: 1. Atomic energy industries.
      2. Atomic energy industries—Safety measures.
      3. Atomic energy—Moral and religious aspects.

HCL: 1. Nuclear power industries—Security measures.
      2. Nuclear power—Environmental aspects.
      3. Radiation.
      4. Nuclear terrorism.
      5. Nuclear power and civil rights.
      6. Antinuclear movement.

Katz, Arthur M.
Life after nuclear war: the economic and social impact of
nuclear attacks on the United States. 1982.

LC: 1. Atomic warfare—Economic aspects—United
States.
2. Atomic warfare and society—United States.

HCL: 1. Survival (after nuclear warfare).
2. Nuclear warfare—Forecasts.
3. Nuclear warfare—Economic aspects.
4. Nuclear warfare—Social aspects.

Kennedy, Edward M.
Freeze! How you can help prevent nuclear war. 1982.

LC: No record found.

HCL: 1. Nuclear freeze campaign.

Kojm, Christopher A.
The nuclear freeze debate. 1983.

PARTIAL CONTENTS: The origins of the nuclear freeze
movement. -The freeze and START proposals. -Evaluating
the arms control proposals. -The anti-nuclear movement in
Europe.

LC: 1. Atomic weapons—Addresses, essays, lectures.
2. Military policy—Addresses, essays, lectures.
3. Antinuclear movement—United States—
Addresses, essays, lectures.
4. Antinuclear movement—Europe—Addresses,
essays, lectures.

HCL: 1. Nuclear freeze campaign.
2. START (arms control).
3. Antinuclear movement—United States.
4. Antinuclear movement—Europe.
5. Peace movement—Europe.
6. Peace movement—United States.

Last aid: the medical dimensions of nuclear war. 1982.

LC: 1. Radiation—Toxicology—Congresses.

    2. Disaster medicine—Congresses.
    3. Atomic warfare—Congresses.
HCL: 1. Nuclear warfare—Medical aspects.

Lifton, Robert Jay.
Death in life: survivors of Hiroshima. 1957.
LC: 1. Hiroshima—Bombardment, 1945.
    2. Atomic warfare—Psychological aspects.
HCL: 1. Nuclear warfare—Psychological aspects.
    2. Hiroshima—Atomic bombing, 1945.
    3. Hibakusha.

O'Heffernan, Patrick.
The first world nuclear war: a strategy for preventing nuclear wars and the spread of nuclear weapons. 1983.

Jacket subtitle: A frightening scenario of growing Third World nuclear battles threatening atomic holocaust in 1985 unless America changes its definition of national security.

PARTIAL CONTENTS: The Third World nuclear war. -Third World nuclear bomb. Nuclear terrorism. Arms race and the Third World. -Soft path to peace. Nonviolent energy strategies for the Third World.

    LC: 1. Atomic warfare.
         2. World War III.
         3. Atomic energy industries.
         4. Nuclear nonproliferation.
         5. Atomic weapons and disarmament.
         6. Energy policy.
    HCL: 1. Nuclear warfare—Forecasts.
         2. National security—United States.
         3. Military forecasting.
         4. Nuclear weapons—Third World.
         5. Nuclear terrorism—Third World.
         6. Energy policy—Third World.
         7. World War III (projected).
         8. Nuclear holocaust—Forecasts.
         9. Arms race.
        10. Nuclear nonproliferation.

Pauling, Linus.
No more war! 1983.

PARTIAL CONTENTS: Radioactivity and fallout. -Radiation and heredity. -Radiation and disease. -The scientists appeal for peace. -A proposal: research for peace.

LC: 1. Atomic weapons and disarmament.
2. Atomic weapons.

HCL: 1. Nuclear warfare.
2. Nuclear disarmament.
3. Scientists—Social responsibility.
4. Radiation—Health hazards.
5. Peace research.

Pomerantz, Charlotte.
The princess and the admiral. 1974.

LC: 1. East (Far East)—Fiction.

HCL: 1. Peace—Fiction.
2. Sex role—Fiction.
3. War stories.
4. Princesses—Fiction.
5. Sexism—Fiction.
6. Cleverness—Fiction.
7. Jan Addams Children's Book Award Winners.
8. Nonsexist children's literature.
9. Asia—Fiction.

Saffer, Thomas H.
Countdown zero. 1982.

LC: 1. Atomic weapons—Testing.
2. Veterans—Diseases—United States.
3. Atomic bomb—Physiological effect.
4. Ionizing radiation—Physiological effect.
5. United States—Armed forces—History—20th Century.

HCL: 1. Atomic bomb—Testing.
2. Atomic veterans.
3. Veterans—Diseases.
4. Atomic bomb—Human effects.

    5. Radiation—Health hazards.
    6. Nuclear power and cancer.

Scheer, Robert.
    With enough shovels: Reagan, Bush and nuclear war. 1982.

    PARTIAL CONTENTS: Nuke war—and birds. -Window of vulnerability. -Civil defense.

    LC: 1. Atomic warfare.
          2. United States—Military policy.
          3. United States—Politics and government—
             1981- .

    HCL: 1. Reagan, Ronald, 1911- .
          2. Bush, George.
          3. Civil defense.
          4. Nuclear warfare.
          5. Nuclear weapons policy.

Schell, Jonathan.
    The fate of the earth. 1982.

    LC: 1. Atomic warfare.

    HCL: 1. Nuclear warfare.
          2. Nuclear weapons.
          3. Nuclear disarmament.

Shaheen, Jack G.
    Nuclear war films. 1978.

    LC: 1. War films—History and criticism.
          2. Atomic warfare in motion pictures.

    HCL: 1. Nuclear war films—History and criticism.

Uhl, Michael.
    GI guinea pigs: how the Pentagon exposed our troops to dangers more deadly than war: Agent Orange and atomic radiation. 1980.

    LC: 1. Veterans—United States—Diseases.
          2. Atomic bomb—Physiological effect.
          3. Radiation—Toxicology.

        4. Herbicides—War use.
        5. Herbicides—Toxicology.
HCL: 1. Veterans—Diseases.
        2. Vietnam veterans—Diseases.
        3. Atomic veterans.
        4. Disabled veterans.
        5. Agent Orange.
        6. Military accountability.
        7. Radiation—Health hazards.
        8. United States. Veterans Administration.

Vanderhaar, Gerard A.
Christians and nonviolence in the nuclear age: scripture,
the arms race, and you. 1982.

LC: No record found.

HCL: 1. Nuclear warfare—Moral and ethical aspects.
        2. Nuclear weapons—Moral and ethical aspects.
        3. Arms race—Moral and ethical aspects.
        4. Nonviolence.
        5. Christianity and peace.

Wilcox, Fred.
Grass roots: an anti-nuke source book. 1980.

PARTIAL CONTENTS: How to form a grass roots organization. -How to use civil disobedience to oppose nuclear
power. -How to start an initiative petition.

LC: 1. Atomic energy policy—United States—
            Citizen participation.
        2. Politics, Practical.

HCL: 1. Civil disobedience.
        2. Antinuclear movement—Organizing
            handbooks, manuals, etc.
        3. Practical politics.
        4. Grassroots movement—Organizing
            handbooks, manuals, etc.

Conclusion: Current orthodox subject cataloging of material on
war, peace, and nuclear holocaust suffers from three serious
defects:

1. It doesn't facilitate "first hits," largely due to petrified language (e.g., "Atomic" instead of "Nuclear").
2. It fails to recognize and legitimize specific new topics (e.g., "Nuclear freeze campaign," "Limited nuclear war," "Peace conversion").
3. It fails to provide sufficient access points for multi-topic works (e.g., O'Heffernan, Pomerantz).

What can be done about it? Two things:

1. Suggest reforms to The Chief, Subject Cataloging Division, The Library of Congress, Washington, DC 20540.
2. Implement reforms locally, as HCL has done.

To empower the public with vital information on such grave and immediate subjects should be a top library priority. And that includes swift and accurate catalog access.

Authority Control: Issues and Answers

Doris Hargrett Clack

INTRODUCTION

Interest in authority control is intensifying and becoming more widespread as libraries advance from the traditional manual catalog to the online catalog. Before the advent of online catalogs, many libraries merely paid lip service to the concept of authority control; others saw little need to allocate already scarce resources to such activity and never thought of it as a priority.

Once the computer was introduced into the cataloging process, it became a common belief that all bibliographic retrieval problems would be solved. There was a misconception that integrity of the catalog was not necessary for an online catalog. Some libraries attempted to convert uncontrolled bibliographic data from their old manual files into machine-readable form to produce an online catalog. It was believed that with the computer a catalog could be produced that would be flexible and that could retrieve any information as long as it was in machine-readable form. Of course, these misconceptions proved to be very costly and resulted in a reprioritizing of library activities. The computer does provide the online catalog with considerable flexibility; however, flexibility without the type of integrity generated by authority control does not make for a very efficient file.

Definition

What is authority control: It is a technical process that is executed on a library catalog. When properly carried out, it provides the underlying structure of the catalog. Uniqueness, standardization, the linkage are the foundation of authority control.

Authority control works through an authority file that contains the terms used as access points in a catalog. The access points may be

127

real entry headings or cross references. The entry headings determine the structure of the catalog. In library catalogs the entry headings that are under control generally consist of personal and corporate names, uniform titles, series, and subjects.

A particular set of operations must be carried out on every name, uniform title, series, or subject before it is ready to go into the catalog as an access point. The operation involves research, the creation of standardized forms of access points, and linkages to variant forms of those access points. Without initial, meticulous research, a name cannot be judged unique, distinguishable from other names that are already in the catalog or that may be candidates for inclusion at some later date. The process requires a lot of time and professional judgement.

Schmierer says that the decisions in determining access points and the recording of those decisions about the choices may be defined as authority control. She lists three major activities associated with authority control:

1. collecting, recording, and maintaining authority data,
2. verifying,
3. using established authorized forms as access points in the catalog.[1]

Experts in the field seem to be in general agreement as to what authority control really is. Hagler and Simmons define authority control as "the name given to the function of discovering all available evidence relative to the naming of a person, body, topic, etc., and then establishing an access point and cross-references according to some rule."[2] Avram says "authority control is a process for insuring consistency of headings in a library catalog."[3] Martin defines it as "the set of procedures which determines the use of consistent names and terminology in the face of pseudonyms, changing names; changing subject terminology; and changing relationships between and among scholarly disciplines, corporate bodies and governmental agencies."[4] From Elias comes this definition: "Authority control is the process by which the same or related names, phrases, or titles are brought together in a particular place in the catalog."[5]

Summarily, authority control is the process of insuring that every entry—name, uniform title, series, or subject—that is selected as an access point for the public catalog is unique and does not conflict, by being identical, with any other entry that is already in the catalog or that may be included at a later date. A network of "see" and "see also" references is the frame that ties it all together.

Purpose

To understand the purpose of authority control, one must first be familiar with the nature of library catalogs, what their primary functions are, and how they are put together to ensure that those functions are carried out expeditiously.

In 1876 Charles Ammi Cutter characterized a catalog as "merely an index to the library, giving in the shortest possible compass clues by which the public can find books."[6] He went on to enumerate the functions of the catalog. His objects are classic statements of the functions that library catalogs are expected to fulfill:

1. To enable a person to find a book of which either the author, title or subject is known.
2. To show what the library has by a given author, on a given subject, in a given kind of literature.
3. To assist in the choice of a book as to its edition (bibliographically); as to its character (literary or topical).[7]

The Council of Library Resources' working definition of a catalog is as follows: "a set of bibliographic records under control of authority files which describes a set of resources contained in collections, libraries, networks, and so forth. It is the instrument by which bibliographic control is maintained and by which the relationship between individual bibliograhic records can be indicated. . .The catalog may include other types of records as well, such as cross-references and on-order information."[8]

Taking into consideration Cutter's *objects,* library catalogs serve two basic functions. The first function helps a user learn what materials are in the library and where they are located. This is known as the finding function. In order for the catalog to fulfill this function, it must offer access to the names of authors, titles, and subjects stored there. This function satisfies the needs of those users searching for a simple, discrete item. It, however, can satisfy the needs of library users only part of the time. If a user knows a particular name of an author, a search of the catalog under that name will allow that user to find the work if, indeed, the library owns a copy. The same holds true if a particular title or the subject of a particular work is known. A search of the catalog under the particular title or subject will allow the user to find the material if it is in the library's collection.

The finding function emphasizes the individual bibliographic record. Bibliographic records are surrogates for the items they describe. Each description represents a unique, physical item in the collection. The creation of individual bibliographic records involves a mechanical process of following a prescribed set of rules, *AACR2*. With an agreed upon set of standards and the physical item in hand, there is little disagreement on what represents an acceptable description. Trained professionals can easily create unique bibliographic records that can unambiguously identify an item in a collection. The rules have been internationally accepted and, with minor variations, result in fairly uniform descriptions around the globe.

The second function of the catalog is to enable the display of the works of a given author, works on a given subject, and the manifestation of various editions of a work. This is known as collocation or the gathering function. Of the two functions authority control is more closely related to this one than to the other.

The gathering function satisifies the majority of the needs of users a majority of the time. It helps the user who approaches the catalog with incomplete information. A user may know a particular name used by an author. The author, however, may have written under several different names and/or may have used several different forms of a name. A library may choose to use every name or it may choose to use only one of the many names associated with the author. In order to find a particular item by the author, the user will come to the library not fully equipped with either of these pieces of information about the author. To facilitate the user's search the library will need a reference network of variant names linked together to assure that the user gets complete information. The linking in the network of references may be visible as in a manual catalog or it may be transparent as in an online catalog.

The consistency resulting from linkage and collocation is the function of authority control. Such controlled files with clearly established linking access points are much easier to use than uncontrolled files because they do not make too many academic demands upon the user.

Collocation emphasizes entry headings and reference structure. The choice and form of entry, like bibliographic description, are based on *AACR2*. More intellectual judgement, however, is required to make effective choices than is required to create a bibliographic description.

Every record in the catalog is related to the others. This relationship is made obvious through a network of references that supports the structure of the catalog. The organization and structure of the catalog affect its usefulness. Library users cannot expect to know the rules of choice and form of entry that provide structure; therefore, it is essential that the structure be consistent and readily apparent. Continuity of the structure must exist if the catalog is to retain its effectiveness.

Collocation brings together all editions of a work owned by a library. A work may become known by various titles since publishers do not necessarily use the same title for a work. During the cataloging process, the identity of the work is captured and labelled to facilitate the collocation or gathering function. A uniform title may be assigned as the gathering device for relating the various editions of the work.

Library users will usually request any undefined edition of a work instead of a particular edition. They may not know the specific edition needed or they may not know that other editions are available if editions are not collocated in the catalog. Some users may be fully satisfied if they get any one of several manifestations of a particular work. Others may want or need a particular edition. An effective catalog will reveal to them all the editions of a work which equally meet their needs or which could meet their needs better. They are better served when the catalog brings to their attention related editions about which they may not have known initially.

Some users may erroneously assume that the library does not own a particular edition of a work if it is not displayed in the catalog or on the shelf along with the others. They may even assume that it does not exist at all. It may not occur to them that the various editions have not been efficiently collocated. They may not be aware of the existence of other editions that could very well serve their needs if the edition sought is out on loan or is not on the shelf for some other reason. Collocation gives them choices from which they may make satisfactory substitutions when the edition they seek is not available. Some industrious user may attempt a truly thorough search and waste very valuable time browsing an uncontrolled catalog since there is no way to know when an unsuccessful search should be terminated.

Series authority files document the decisions concerning accepted practice. They provide a record of established precedence of treatment. It is important for library users to be able to have all parts of a series follow the same treatment whether the decision is to group them all under the series title and classify them together as a collection or to disperse them throughout the collection. Ensuring this uniformity in treatment is the function of series authority control.

Theoretically, the function of subject authority control is to ensure the use of consistent vocabulary that exactly matches both that of the user and that of the document. In practice authority control ensures the consistency in the vocabulary and the reference structure used in the library. If the terms from the controlled vocabulary are properly assigned to documents, then authority control ensures that all materials on a given subject are collocated under the same subject term. The adequacy of any subject authority control system is as much dependent upon the quality of application as it is upon the quality of the system itself.

Major Issues

With the introduction of any new procedure or product of the magnitude of authority control and online catalogs, unresolved issues will only naturally surface. With an increase in the number of online catalogs being used or planned for, libraries are having to reassess their positions on authority control. As a result numerous issues have been raised—both theoretical and practical. There is no doubt that new issues will continue to arise even as old ones are resolved. Just as no list of issues can be considered complete, no solution offered can be considered the only one that works. So, what are the major issues?

Is Authority Control Really Necessary?

The flurry of activity going on at the national level with regard to the establishment of a national authority file service suggests that local libraries have no need to be concerned with authority control. A cooperative system that links the databases of the Library of Congress with those of WLN, RLG, and OCLC (tentative) has just been inaugurated. A library that belongs to one of the three major bibliographic utilities will, indeed, have the advantage of having their bibliographic records validated automatically for the proper form of access points before adding them to the data base. This validation will ensure a controlled file at the local level.

To suggest that libraries at the local level need not be concerned about authority control because of the linked file service is to fail to consider the nature and the needs of hundreds of libraries that are not affiliated with a bibliographic utility. There are more than 29,500 academic, public, and special libraries in the United States,[9] of which 130 are affiliated with WLN, 30 with RLG/RLIN, and approximately 3,700 with OCLC.[10] That leaves more than 25,000 libraries outside the linked system. The contents of the linked authority file will be available in formats other than online such as microform and paper, thus making access to the national files available to other libraries.

Data in authority files do not remain static. They are dynamic and in a constant state of change. For a library to make adequate use of the national files, knowledge of the functions of authority control is mandatory. A thorough understanding of procedures and practices of authority work is also necessary. One must be aware of the areas of potential problems and workable solutions.

Even if the basic authority information is available from the national files, such information must be transferred to a local catalog to meet local needs. Libraries at the local level certainly do need to be concerned about authority control.

Is Authority Control Really Necessary in an Online Environment?

Since the computer can be programmed to create many different displays from a wide variety of search keys, the question has been raised: Is authority control necessary at all in an online system? Interestingly enough, it was the advent of online catalogs that created a renewed interest in authority control in the first place.

The computer can retrieve information rapidly and accurately. It is not necessarily dependent upon entry words, linear order, or static formats. Its flexibility is one of its greatest assets. So why authority control?

The speed, accuracy, and flexibility that characterize the capability of the computer are the results of human intervention. The decisions about what constitutes a personal name for a particular individual is predetermined by a human mind. Prior knowledge of the varied names, the order of the words in the names, the links that tie them all together is a human judgement. That is authority control.

The manipulation of that data is all the computer does. Admittedly, it does so extremely well.

How Much Imposed Standardization Is Enough?

Some libraries maintain very accurate authority files. Others are just beginning to consider them for the first time. The question of standardization has been raised as a concern. Some librarians feel that standardization at the national level is being imposed on libraries at the expense of local needs. With a national file service in place, there will be little need for local libraries to duplicate authority work done at the national level. The changes in names discovered at the national level are valid for libraries in the local level. Chances are that a national level authority record will be the fullest possible and will be undergoing constant review and updating as more information is discovered that affects the data in the file. Individual libraries may find that national level records contain information that would be irrelevant in their catalogs. A library may find that it can omit certain bits of irrelevant information without reducing the integrity of the catalog. Some libraries may find it difficult to integrate all forms of entries used in the national file into their own catalogs.

The issue of relinquishing local needs for the sake of national standards will need to be carefully analyzed and all factors considered. Cost factors, convenience, and probable impact on service to users should be of primary importance.

Is Choosing an Authorized Form of Name Obsolete?

Authority control usually implies one authorized form of name for a personal author under which all works of that author are collocated. Is it really necessary to select one form of an author's name? This is a question that has not been fully answered. In a manual catalog the practice of using uniform entry headings will save the time of the user who wishes a particular work by an author. A systematically arranged file of titles under a single name may be browsed more rapidly than a file of titles scattered throughout the catalog under various names. Either arrangement will require references to link the various names. Linking the various names will assure that an author's name is located regardless of the name used to enter the file.

In an online environment there is no need for a single authorized name or form of name. Links between names, however, are still necessary to show which names belong to which individual. The computer can be programmed to bring together works by an author under each name used. This action can be rapid, accurate, and transparent. A user could make a single query under either of the varied names and the computer would do the rest. Bibliographic data that reside in a computer memory have no structure that is relevant to a searcher until it is displayed at the end of a search. The presentation of the data can take many forms and is solely dependent upon the programming that creates the display.

How Much External Influence Is Enough?

Should a library change its name authority files to fit the system from an outside source? There are advantages and disadvantages. To keep the local system intact eliminates the need to change headings already established to meet local needs. Only the new entries would need to be changed in cases of conflict between the choices of the two systems. Time can be saved since no time will need to be expanded in searching to determine the entry used by the outside source.

These advantages may be outweighed, however, by the fact that participation in a network is impossible if a library chooses not to change its name authority file to fit the system of the network. A library may choose to give up its local authority file in order to participate in a network. It may be necessary, however, to change a great many entries initially in order for the files to be merged. Also the library will lose control over decisions regarding any future modifications to the system. Advantages and disadvantages will vary from library to library, depending on how closely the library adheres to the latest cataloging rules, how many local variations the local system requires, and how willing the library is to give up its autonomy.

Can Authority Control Be Provided for Shared Databases?

The move from manual catalogs to online catalogs and the development of shared bibliographic databases are raising important questions about how best to provide authority control for such shared databases. It is difficult to impose authority control over shared databases because of the lack of uniformity in the files. Some libraries use non-traditional methods of authority control while others have bibliographic files that were created under no authority control. Authority control of shared databases is likely to remain a major problem for years to come.

How Successful Is Authority Control at Remote Sites?

Some libraries that are part of a network or system are developing their own individual automated authority control system. Authority records can now be stored in the computer at remote sites. They may be maintained, administered, and controlled by one organization at yet another site while other organizations use and contribute to the system. The questions with the broadest implications that have been raised concern the maintenance of the systems authority files once the local authority system is up and running. Should they coexist? Or should they merge? If they are merged, who should maintain, administer, control, or even contribute to the file? Funding and location of the experts will decide the answers to many of the questions raised.

What Kind of Reference System Is Best in an Online Authority System?

The reference structure of the first dictionary catalogs correlated name/title to name/title according to procedures established by Charles Ammi Cutter. A brief bibliographic record was a part of every reference. In attempts to streamline the catalog and to make it more efficient in its manual form, the reference structure was changed to a name to name reference structure. The user was deprived of the convenience of being able to associate immediately an author with his work when entering the catalog at the point of a variant name. Now the reference structure based on entry rather than record is being automated. Authors' names will be manipulated without any accompanying bibliographic record. No doubt this will be the standard structure of online authority systems.

The entry method raises some valid questions about the approach and about valid alternatives. It may be useful in a manual system but has no place in an online system. The capabilities of the computer are too powerful to settle for this type of reference system. Anything less than a full accounting of an author's works under every name should be rejected.

Is Quality Control Possible?

Quality control in authority files is as much an issue as quality control of bibliographic records was before the advent of networking in libraries. Libraries can get high quality bibliographic records from a wide variety of sources. The bibliographic utilities are able to select high quality records or improve on those that are less than ideal. Libraries that depend upon vendors for their bibliographic records, likewise, get good records. Many of the vendors market LC cataloging copy to their customers. Other libraries employ highly trained personnel who are familiar with the cataloging rules and can create high quality records with ease.

Measures for quality control in authority files have not reached the level of quality control for bibliographic records. There are no standards that measure the quality of authority control systems. There is no common understanding of the level of authority control that would best suit a particular type or size of library. Some systems have quality control only for frequently used headings with references. They use simplicity as the basis for inclusion or exclusion. Problems could develop from such criterion since it is difficult, if not impossible, to determine if and/or how long an apparently simple heading will remain so.

Are Integrated Files Better Than Separate Files?

The validity of establishing files by use or type of heading is being questioned. This issue is a primary concern for manual authority files. In an automated environment, there is no question about the value of an integrated authority file system that includes names, series, uniform titles, as well as subjects. In a manual file the division of intrinsic types seems workable if desired. When all types of headings reside in the same file, it becomes more simplified, maintenance is facilitated, and a greater level of uniformity is achieved than when the file is divided. Separate subject authority files may be more tolerable than separate name files. It may be argued that the high frequency of need to use references with subject headings justify separate subject authority files.

In an automated environment manipulating is what the computer does best. Many personal names have as many variants that appear as cross references to the authorized forms of name as may appear with subject headings. In some online catalogs, this procedure works exceptionally well. There is no reason why subject searches cannot be made to be equally as successful. Questions have also been raised regarding the desirability of establishing authority files separate from bibliographic files. Again, there is no reason why they cannot or should not be integrated in an online environment.

What Should be the Standard Components of an Authority System?

The content, style, and format of authority records have not been standardized as yet. Although some minimum standards are developing as a result of the increased concern for authority control in libraries, there is a need to formalize the planning and coordinate the efforts.

The component parts of an authority control system are the record itself and the cross references. The contents of the references are more standardized than are the contents of the record itself. The data most frequently included in an authority record are the established form of heading, the sources of the heading (for names and series), scope notes (for subject headings), and reciprocal references. Some files may have more information but seldom less. Tags and data elements necessary for machine manipulation are also mandatory if the system is automated.

Do the Returns From Establishing and Maintaining Authority Control Justify the Costs?

Rigorous authority control is expensive; however, no control is even more so. Included in the costs of authority control are the time spent in searching, personnel costs, the expense of acquiring and maintaining equipment, the cost of equipment and supplies, typing, proofing, and filing. Costs are also accrued for making changes and resolving conflicts. Many libraries do not consider these as costs because they do not have to be specifically budgeted for. They absorb these costs along with those for normal operational routines.

There is a cost for a successful search by a user and for a failed one. Failure has significant financial implications for a library. An automated system will improve the integrity of the files and will speed up the operations, but, there is no evidence that the actual dollar figures will be reduced. The greatest potential savings to be accrued probably will be in reduced duplication and redundancy.

SUMMARY

Interest in authority control is on the rise, primarily, because of experiences with online catalogs. Before the advances in computer technology made online catalogs possible, only a few libraries were concerned about rigorous authority control over the structure of their manual catalogs. Some gave mere lip service to the idea of authority control. Many more got along without it.

To many libraries authority control is a new concept. As a concept it is a process that ensures that the entry headings in a library catalog are unique and do not conflict with those already in the catalog or with those that may be included at a later date. The entry headings are usually for personal and corporate names, uniform titles, series, and subject headings. Their form and structure create the form and structure of the catalog as a whole. The structure of the catalog should be rigorously controlled to ensure consistency and uniformity which facilitates the use of the catalog by those who are unfamiliar with the rules that determine the entries and, consequently, the structure of the catalog.

Because more libraries are establishing and maintaining authority files than ever before, more attempts at cooperation in authority control—as with bibliographic control—are being made. In beginning any cooperative venture, there will be problems that must be solved before a smooth and effective operation can evolve. Experience and cooperative efforts in authority control have raised numerous issues, many of which remain unresolved. These have ranged from questions about its validity to the best way to do it. Now the computer has created new kinds of problems. There is little doubt, however, that the computer will be instrumental in developing workable solutions and making worthwhile advancements.

It is important that librarians become as knowledgeable as possible about the whole subject of authority control. The excellent bibliography that appears in the January/February issue of *Florida Libraries*[11] and the review article by Larry Auld in the October/December issue of *Library Resources & Technical Services*[12] are two of the best beginnings toward becoming an authority on one of the hottest issues facing the profession today.

REFERENCES

1. Schmierer, Helen, "The Relationship of Authority Control to the Library Catalog," *Illinois Libraries* 62 (Sept. 1980): 602.

2. Hagler, Ronald and Peter Simmons, *The Bibliographic Record and Information Technology.* Chicago: American Library Association, 1982, p. 181.

3. Avram, Henrietta D., "Authority Control and Its Place," *Journal of Academic Librarianship* 9 (1984): 331.

4. Martin, Susan K., "Authority Control: Unnecessary Detail or Needed Support," *Library Issues, Briefings for Faculty and Administrators* 2 (Jan. 1982): 2.

5. Elias, Cathy Ann, and C. James Fair, "Name Authority Control in a Communication System," *Special Libraries* 74 (July 1983): 289.

6. Cutter, Charles Ammi, *Rules for a Dictionary Catalog,* 4th ed., rewritten Washington, D.C.: Government Printing Office, 1904, p. 11.

7. *Ibid.,* p. 12.

8. "An Integrated Consistent Authority File Service for Nationwide Use," *Library of Congress Information Bulletin* 39 (July 11, 1980): 244-248.

9. *American Library Directory,* 37th ed. New York: R.R. Bowker, 1984, v. 1, p. xi.

10. Sources of data: Telephone calls to the three networks on October 8, 1984.

11. Clack, Doris Hargrett, "On Becoming an Authority on Authorities: A Working Bibliography," *Florida Libraries* 33 (Jan./Feb. 1983): 13-18.

12. Auld, Larry, "Authority Control: An Eighty-Year Review," *Library Resources & Technical Services* 26 (Oct./Dec. 1982): 319-330.

Neal Lowndes Edgar
1927-1983

Rosemary D. Harrick

How can one draw an image on paper of an individual's lifetime contributions and how those contributions may have affected the lives of others and librarianship itself. Only in five, twenty-five, or fifty years will librarianship recognize that it has been enriched by Neal Lowndes Edgar's footprints as he strode through the sands of time. But to those of us who were fortunate enough to be both professional associates and friends, we recognize it now.

Neal Lowndes Edgar was born to William John Brown Edgar and Margaret Baker (Thomas) Edgar in New York City on June 27, 1927. Neal was a dedicated librarian for more than twenty-five years, an organizer and an energetic contributor to his chosen profession. He was a researcher and a writer of five books, and he contributed numerous articles and book reviews to professional journals. He was deeply involved in the Kent State University Library, in University activities, and he was an active participant in professional organizations. One of his greatest gifts was his special way of reaching out to all: his peers, his friends and all those persons who were less fortunate, and all gained by this contact.

Undoubtedly Neal was a workaholic, spending long hours in his office and at home in the evenings and on weekends working on his research projects. He had more ideas than his time permitted. Yet he found leisure-time to enjoy recreational reading, classical music, and drama.

While seemingly winning a battle against lung cancer, Neal died unexpectedly on April 2, 1983, succumbing to a heart attack. Neal was but 55 years young, active, dedicated, and creative, with an interest in life and its challenges. He was a student and teacher in his prime.

For most of his life, Neal suffered from a physically deforming disease, von Recklinghausen's disease, or neurofibromatsis. It would have been easy for him to retreat from the world with this debilitating affliction. Instead, he accepted the challenge and fought it by developing a real penchant for learning. This desire for learning was, at least partly, the result of genetics as both of Neal's parents were professionals.

Over a twenty-year period, from 1946-65, his search for learning never ceased, and he earned three master's degrees and a Ph.D. The proofs of his last book, *AACR2 and Serials: American View*, were mailed to the publisher the evening before his death. It was on this evening that Neal participated in a stimulating dialogue with some graduate library science students regarding the principles of the book. It was this type of encounter that gave Neal great joy and pleasure.

Neal became a Converse Scholar in 1947-48 at Trinity College, Hartford, Connecticut, majoring in economics and history. After receiving his AB degree in 1950, Neal became a professional radio broadcaster working in both New York and Massachusetts.

Following a two-year stint as a high school English teacher from 1955-57, he began his library pre-professional work at the New York Academy of Medicine. He next worked as a department assistant at the State University of New York (SUNY) at Albany where he was then simultaneously awarded a double master's degree in both English and librarianship in 1958. After his graduation from SUNY, he became acquisitions librarian at the Hawley Library, SUNY, from 1958-61.

Moving to Ann Arbor, Michigan, he became coordinating librarian for the residence halls at the University of Michigan where he served for four years. While at the University of Michigan, he continued his studies as a Carnegie Scholar during the academic year 1963-64. It was here that he received his third master's degree, completed his Ph.D. in 1965, and met Susanna Jane Capper who was later to become Mrs. Neal Edgar.

Shortly after receiving his Ph.D., Neal moved to Washington, D.C., where he became serials cataloger in the Descriptive Cataloging Division of the Library of Congress. It was in Washington on May 7, 1966, Neal married Susanna, who is also a librarian.

In 1967, the Edgars moved to Kent, Ohio, to the sprawling, rolling, green campus of Kent State University. The following sixteen years Neal was to serve in a wide range of professional appointments. The positions he held included head of acquisitions, head of serials, research librarian, and associate curator of special collections. He was serving as associate curator at the time of his death, working in both rare books and archives departments. It was during this last position that he accepted the challenge of cataloging the rare books arrearage and implementing the *AACR2* cataloging rules he helped devise. In archives he organized and indexed the minutes of the Board of Trustees from the beginnings of the Kent State University when it was known as Kent State Normal College in 1911.

In 1969, when the University librarians received rank and status generally accorded to the teaching faculty, Neal was appointed Associate Professor in Library Administration. It was in 1974 that he was promoted to full Professor of Library Administration. However, Neal had received the distinction of being a professor in library sciences in 1972 where he taught part-time both on the Kent Campus and on the regional campuses for the University's School of Library Science.

Neal admitted in a vita he prepared for the North Central Association that prior to 1975 he had relatively few publications to his credit relating to librarianship. The real turning point in his career was 1977 when he decided that he would seriously turn his attention to research for publication. He felt that with his educational background and wide variety of experience in several academic libraries that there was much he could share with his peers on librarianship. Neal published five books, twelve articles as parts of books, 23 periodical articles, and he had over 44 book reviews to his credit. In addition, Neal served on the editorial board of *Title Varies* for eight years, *The Serials Librarian* for three years, and was a member of the editorial advisory committee for *American Libraries* for two years. He also was serials and periodical review editor for *Ethnic Forum* and reviews editor of *The Serials Librarian.*

Neal was active on University committees and took his commitments seriously. He served three years on both the Student Publications Policy Committee and University Press Editorial Board as an alternate. He served faithfully on the Commencement and Honors Day Committee, University Press Editorial Board, Vice President's Promotions Advisory Board, the Vice President's Tenure Advisory Board, and the Library's Collegial Advisory Committee.

In addition, Neal was in demand as a consultant and worked with Cleveland State University, University Microfilms International, Rochester Regional Research Library Council, Wayne State University Library, and Ohio University Library in a variety of capacities.

Neal became very active in the American Library Association in

1972 where his commitments ranged from serving as chair of the RTSD Serials Section nominating committee to serving a five-year commitment to the RTSD Serials Section on Policy and Research. A special committee activity that should be highlighted was his four-year membership on the RTSD Catalog Code Revision Committee which produced *AACR2*.

Despite Neal's sometimes abrupt, gruff exterior, he was a complex, yet a sensitive, down-to-earth, caring individual. He stimulated and motivated his peers to become interested in doing research for publication. He gave unselfishly of his time and effort to assist those individuals he cared about to help advance their views, thereby advancing their careers. He met his antagonists head-on, showing them there were two sides to every position and that theirs and/or his were not always right. It was Neal's habit to play the devil's advocate for debating purposes in an effort to make people think and to form their opinions on the basis of fact. He thoroughly enjoyed his role. Frequently Neal would bring forth analogies from literature to make his point. Always ready to laugh, Neal loved to laugh at himself and with others; never at others. His laughter was real, robust, and came from deep within him. You could never deny Neal's presence, but that presence was not pretentious. He was an invaluable component in any social gathering, for he could contribute to a rousing conversation on any topic.

In his many years at Kent State, Neal earned from his peers, friends, and adversaries respect as a quality human being. In summary it is fair to say that during his many productive years, he touched many people, and all he touched found that their lives were enriched.

He was a true friend and colleague. Librarianship has been greatly enriched by the life of Neal Lowndes Edgar.

Neal L. Edgar:
A Bibliography of Professional Works

Susan Barnard

Neal Edgar's professional works present an extensive cross section of inquiry into contemporary topics in the field of librarianship. His expertise was best developed in the areas of serials and cataloging; perhaps his most notable contributions were his dissertation and book on early nineteenth-century American magazines, and his service on the *AACR2* catalog code revision committee. But, as this list of publications shows, Neal's eclectic professional curiosity led him into a number of other realms as well: preservation, bibliography, collection development, automation. In fact, there are few dimensions of librarianship in which he did not sustain some interest, or could not comment upon reliably. To his credit, his considerable knowledge of his own specialties did not obstruct his perspective on other library matters, nor obscure his understanding of the interdependence of them all. He was a technical services practitioner who remained cognizant of public needs, and of the library's fundamental mission of serving users.

Neal's writing style, clear and straightforward, reflects his nononsense way of thinking. In an attempt to characterize the publishing nature of serials, he concisely observed, "a serial continues and a serial changes." He detested pretension in any context, but particularly in formal writing. Among his frequent targets was the use of affected academic jargon, which he dubbed "educationese." Although Neal seemed to delight in exposing exaggeration, inconsistency and misrepresentation, as some authors whose books were reviewed by him experienced, his motives were not malicious. Rather, he approached his own work with absolute honesty and integrity, and he expected no less of others. He courted a curmudgeonly reputation, but this image was softened by an alert sense of humor

145

and unfailing compassion. For one so well-acquainted with suffering, Neal's characteristic equanimity and ready delight in commonplace circumstances were inspirational.

The several years preceding Neal's death were ones of accelerated productivity and, although he lived only three months into 1983, that year witnessed the publication of two major works. In the final months of his life, when his capacity for work was diminished, he expressed frustration because he saw so much work to be done and he simply could not perform tirelessly, as was his custom. His illness was a bothersome interference, but he persisted. Within hours of his death, he return-mailed the proofs of his last book, *AACR2 and Serials: The American View,* to its publisher.

This bibliography of Neal's work is arranged into the following sections: separate publications—original works, separate publications—edited works, parts of books, articles, book reviews, indexes, and reviews of books authored by Neal. Entries are in chronological order, from earliest to latest, within each section.

SEPARATE PUBLICATIONS—ORIGINAL WORKS

Les Journaux Clandestins, 1940-1945: A Reel Guide. Kent, OH: Kent State University Library. Serials Department, 1971.

A History and Bibliography of American Magazines, 1810-1820. Metuchen, NJ: Scarecrow Press, 1975.

The OCLC Serials Sub-system: A First Evaluation, with Wendy Yu Ma and Verna Lanham. Arlington, VA: Computer Microfilm International, 1980.

Travel in Asia: A Guide to Information Sources, with Wendy Yu Ma. Detroit, MI: Gale Research Company, 1983.

SEPARATE PUBLICATIONS—EDITED WORKS

AACR2 and Its Impact on Libraries: Papers Presented at the Academic Library Association of Ohio Annual Meeting and Conference, Worthington, Ohio, October, 1979. Columbus, OH: Ohio State University Libraries. Publications Committee, 1980.

AACR2 and Serials: The American View. New York: The Haworth Press, 1983.

PARTS OF BOOKS

"Labor and Industrial Relations." In *Magazines for Libraries*, 2nd ed., by Bill Katz, 454-457. New York: Bowker, 1972.

_____. Supplement, 156-158. New York: Bowker, 1974.

"The Image of Librarianship in the Media." In *A Century of Service: Librarianship in the United States and Canada*, edited by Sidney Jackson, Eleanor Herling and E.J. Josey, 303-320. Chicago: American Library Association, 1976.

Anglo-American Cataloging Rules, 2nd ed. Chicago: American Library Association, 1978. (Contributed as member of the Catalog Code Revision Committee.)

"Labor and Industrial Relations." In *Magazines for Libraries*, 3rd ed., by Bill Katz, 512-517. New York: Bowker, 1978.

"AACR2 and Serials Cataloging." In *Proceedings of the 2nd AACR 2 Conference Held at Hobart and William Smith Colleges, June, 1979*. Geneva, NY: Hobart and William Smith Colleges, 1979.

100 annotations in 14 subject areas, In *Serials for Libraries: An Annotated Guide to Continuations, Annuals, Yearbooks, Transactions, Proceedings, Directories, Services*, by Joan K. Marshall. New York: Neal/Schumann, 1979.

"Impact of AACR 2 on Serials and Analysis." In *The Making of a Code: The Issues Underlying AACR 2*, edited by Doris H. Clack, 88-105. Chicago: American Library Association, 1980.

"Books and Book Reviews" and "Labor and Industrial Relations." In *Magazines for Libraries*, 4th ed., edited by Bill Katz, 173-187, 532-541. New York: Bowker, 1982.

"Computer Cataloging for Serials: Ramblings of a Curmudgeon." In *The Management of Serials Automation*, edited by Peter Gellatly, 119-134. New York: The Haworth Press, 1982.

"Introduction." In *Introduction to Serials Management*, by Marcia Tuttle, xxi-xxviii. Greenwich, CT: JAI Press, 1982.

ARTICLES

"Benjamin Franklin: A Bibliographic Note." *The Serif* 4 (December 1967): 30.

"What Every Librarian Should Know About Changes in Cataloging Rules: A Brief Overview." *American Libraries* 6 (November 1975): 602-607.

"Code Revision." *Title Varies* 3, no. 1 (January 1976): 4.

"Serials Entry: Quo Vadis?" *Title Varies* 3, no. 2 (March 1976): 5, 7-9.

"Catalog Code Revision Update." *Title Varies* 3, no. 5 (September 1976): 31, 35.

"ALAO Annual Conference Summary." *Academic Library Association of Ohio Quarterly Newsletter* (December 1976): 1-4.

"Some Implications of Code Revision for Serials Librarians." *The Serials Librarian* 1 (Winter 1976/1977): 125-134.

"Title Madness: Another Absorbing Example." *Title Varies* 4, no. 2 & 3 (March/May 1977): 19.

"ISBD(S): A Descriptive Evaluation." *Title Varies* 4, nos. 4-6 (July/November 1977): 33-34.

"Library Periodical Literature: A Centennial Assessment." *The Serials Librarian* 2 (Summer 1978): 341-350.

With Karen Brewer and Gary Pitkin. "A Method for Cooperative Serials Selection and Cancellation Through Consortium Activities." *The Journal of Academic Librarianship* 4 (September 1978): 204-208.

"Freezing the Catalog: A Discussion Paper." *Alternative Catalog Newsletter* 7 (October 1978): 41-50.

"Newsletters for Networks." *Serials Review* 5 (October/December 1979): 61-67.

"Some Thoughts in Response to Lanier and Anderson." *The Serials Librarian* 6 (Fall 1981): 95-98.

"Computers and Libraries." *Ashtabula Campus Current* no. 3 (18 November 1981): 3-4, 6-8.

"New Fields." *The Reference Librarian* no. 1/2 (Fall/Winter 1981): 147-148.

"Missing Issues: One Technique for Replacement." *Library Acquisitions: Practice and Theory* 6 (1982): 295-300.

"Pamphlets in Special Collections." *Friends of the Kent State University Libraries Newsletter* 10 (Fall 1982): 3-4.

"Periodicals and Serials." *Ethnic Forum* 2 (Fall 1982): 109-113.

With Rosemary D. Harrick. "Thoughts on Policy Manuals for Reference Services." *The Reference Librarian* no. 3 (Fall 1982): 55-59.

"Technical Services in Ten Years." *Technical Services Quarterly* 1 (Fall/Winter 1983): 11-18.

"Andrew Osborn: The Father of Serials Librarianship." *Technical Services Quarterly* 1 (Spring 1984): 55-61.

BOOK REVIEWS

"Library Acquisitions: Practice and Theory." *Title Varies* 3 (November 1976): 41.

"The Serials Librarian." *Title Varies* 3 (November 1976): 40.

"Moment." *Library Journal* 101 (December 15, 1976): 2555.

"A Practical Approach to Serials Cataloging," by Lynn S. Smith. *Library Journal* 103 (December 1, 1978): 2395-2396. Also, *Serials Librarian* 3 (Summer 1979): 429-431.

"The Library As a Learning Service Center," by Patrick R. Penland and Aleyamma Mathai. *ARBA 79* no. 153.

"Subject Description of Books: A Manual of Procedures for Augmenting Subject Descriptions in Library Catalogs," edited by Barbara Settel. *ARBA 79* no. 282.

"Preservation of Paper and Textiles of Historic and Artistic Value," edited by John C. Williams. *Serials Review* 5 (January/March 1979): 56-57.

"Periodicals Administration in Libraries: A Collection of Essays," edited by Paul Mayes. *College and Research Libraries* 40 (March 1979): 171-172.

"Victorian Periodicals: A Guide to Research," by Scott Bennett et al. *College and Research Libraries* 40 (March 1979): 191-192.

"ISBD(S): International Standard Bibliographic Description for

Serials," by the International Federation of Library Associations. *Library Resources and Technical Services* 23 (Spring 1979): 184-187.

"Development of a Responsive Library Acquisitions Formula: Final Report," by the State University of New York. Office of Library Services. *Library Journal* 104 (November 1, 1979): 2291.

"The Bibliography of Museum and Art Gallery Publications and Audio-Visual Aids in Great Britain and Ireland 1977," edited by Jean Lambert. *ARBA 80* no. 18.

"The Periodicals Collection," by Donald Davinson. *ARBA 80* no. 151.

"The Little Magazine in America: A Modern Documentary History," edited by Elliott Anderson and Mary Kinzie. *Serials Review* 6 (April/June 1980): 59-60.

"A Comparative Evaluation of Alternative Systems for the Provision of Effective Access to Periodical Literature: A Report to the National Commission on Libraries and Information Science," by Arthur D. Little, Inc. *College and Research Libraries* 41 (May 1980): 251-253.

"Analysis of the 1977 University of California Union List of Serials," by Barbara Radke and Mike Berger. *College and Research Libraries* 41 (July 1980): 386-387.

"Free Magazines for Libraries," by Adeline Mercer Smith. *Library Journal* 105 (November 15, 1980): 2392.

"Alternatives in Print: An International Catalog of Books, Pamphlets, Periodicals and Audiovisual Materials," 6th ed., by the Task Force on Alternatives in Print. *ARBA 81* no. 87.

"College Alumni Publications," by Richard Weiner and James F. Colasurdo. *ARBA 81* no. 27.

"Corporate Publications in Prints," edited by Craig T. Norback. *ARBA 81* no. 8.

"The Librarian's Psychological Commitments: Human Relations in Librarianship," by Florence DeHart. *ARBA 81* no. 122.

"Topics, Terms and Research Techniques: Self-Instruction in

Using Library Catalogs," by Richard T. Strawn. *ARBA 81* no. 255.

"Serial Publications: Their Place and Treatment in Libraries," by Andrew D. Osborn. *Library Journal* 106 (February 1, 1981): 315. Also, *Serials Review* 7 (April/June 1981): 62-64.

"A.L.A. Filing Rules" and "Library of Congress Filing Rules," a combined review. *College and Research Libraries* 42 (July 1981): 389-391.

"Corporate Authorship: Its Role in Library Cataloging," by Michael Carpenter. *Library Journal* 107 (November 15, 1981): 2219.

"Basic Library Skills: A Short Course," by Carolyn E. Wolf and Richard Wolf. *ARBA 82* no. 284.

"Bookbinding & Conservation by Hand: A Working Guide," by Laura S. Young. *ARBA 82* no. 273.

"Cataloging and Classification Quarterly." *ARBA 82* no. 241.

"Evaluation and Training for Information Services in Business and Industry in Developing and Developed Countries," by the International Federation for Documentation. *ARBA 82* no. 275.

"An Introduction to PRECIS for North American Usage," by Phyllis A. Richmond. *ARBA 82* no. 251.

"Stack Management: A Practical Guide to Shelving and Maintaining Library Collections," by William J. Hubbard. *ARBA 82* no. 299.

"Building Blocks in Ethnic Resources: A Preliminary Guide," by David Reith. *Ethnic Forum* 2 (Spring 1982): 89-90.

"Legislative History of American Immigration Policy, 1798-1965," by E.P. Hutchinson. *Ethnic Forum* 2 (Spring 1982): 75-77.

"Serials Automation for Acquisition and Inventory Control," edited by William Gray Potter and Arlene Farber Sirkin. *Library Journal* 107 (June 1, 1982): 1076.

"A History of the Mexican-American People," by Julian Samora and Patricia Vandel Simon. *Ethnic Forum* 2 (Fall 1982): 94-95.

"Special Collections in the Library of Congress," by Annette Melville. *Ethnic Forum* 2 (Fall 1982): 107-108.

"The Bloomsbury Review." *Library Journal* 107 (October 1, 1982): 1833.

"Openers." *Library Journal* 107 (October 15, 1982): 1957.

"Head & Hand: A Socialist Review of Books." *Library Journal* 107 (November 1, 1982): 2155.

"The Pathfinder." *Library Journal* 107 (November 1, 1982): 2057.

"Caving: The Sierra Club Guide to Spelunking," by Lane Larson and Peggy Larson. *ARBA 83* no. 665.

"The Conservation of Archival and Library Materials: A Resource Guide to Audiovisual Aids," by Alice W. Harrison, Edward A. Collister and R. Ellen Willis. *ARBA 83* no. 213.

"Directory of American Preservation Commissions," edited by Stephen N. Dennis. *ARBA 83* no. 378.

"Library of Congress Classification Schedules: Indexes to Class P Subclasses and to Their Additions and Changes through 1978," edited by Helen Savage. *ARBA 83* no. 185.

"Protecting Your Collection: A Handbook, Survey & Guide for the Security of Rare Books, Manuscripts, Archives and Works of Art," by Slade Richard Gandert. *ARBA 83* no. 212.

"Rare Book Librarianship," by Roderick Cave. *ARBA 83* no. 163.

"Reading Research and Librarianship: A History and Analysis," by Stephen Karetzky. *ARBA 83* no. 225.

"A Selective Bibliography on the Conservation of Research Library Materials," by Paul N. Banks. *ARBA 83* no. 109.

"Alternative Papers: Selections from the Alternative Press, 1979-1980," edited by Elliott Shore et al. *Newsletter on Intellectual Freedom* 32 (January 1983): 5-6, 23.

"Automating Library Acquisitions: Issues and Outlooks," by Richard W. Boss. *Library Journal* 108 (January 15, 1983): 114.

"PRECIS: A Workbook for Students of Librarianship," by Michael J. Ramsden. *Serials Librarian* 7 (Spring 1983): 71-72.

"Theory of Library Classification," by Brian Buchanan. *Serials Librarian* 7 (Spring 1983): 69-70.

INDEXES

"The Serif: Eleven Year Cumulative Index, 1964-1974." *The Serif* 11 (Winter 1975): 54-73.

"Index to Volume XXIII (1977)." *Civil War History* 23 (December 1977): 373-381.

"Index to Volume XXIV (1978)." *Civil War History* 24 (December 1978): 368-378.

"Index to Volume XXV (1979)." *Civil War History* 25 (December 1979): 371-382.

"Index to Volume XXVI (1980)." *Civil War History* 26 (December 1980): 368-378.

"Index to Volume XXVII (1981)." *Civil War History* 27 (December 1981): 377-388.

"Index to Volume XXVIII (1982)." *Civil War History* 28 (December 1982): 361-380.

REVIEWS OF BOOKS AUTHORED BY NEAL L. EDGAR

Review of *A History and Bibliography of American Magazines, 1810-1820. ARBA 76* no. 1162.

Review of *A History and Bibliography of American Magazines, 1810-1820. Library Journal* 101 (February 1, 1976): 516.

Katz, Bill. "LJ: Magazines." Comments on *A History and Bibliography of American Magazines, 1810-1820. Library Journal* 101 (April 15, 1976): 991.

Shotwell, Richard. Review of *A History and Bibliography of American Magazines, 1810-1820. RQ* 15 (Spring 1976): 270.

Review of *A History and Bibliography of American Magazines, 1810-1820. Choice* 13 (May 1976): 346.

Sheehy, Eugene. "Selected Reference Books of 1975-76." Review of *A History and Bibliography of American Magazines, 1810-1820. College and Research Libraries* 37 (July 1976): 358.

Review of *A History and Bibliography of American Magazines, 1810-1820. Booklist* 73 (September 1, 1976): 56.

Review of *Travel in Asia: A Guide to Information Sources. Choice* 20 (July-August 1983): 1573.

Black, Sophie K. Review of *AACR2 and Serials: The American View. Booklist* 80 (January 15, 1984): 714.

Contributors

SUSAN BARNARD is a reference librarian at the Kent State University Library. Her previous library positions include that of assistant at the Congressional Quarterly Library in Washington, D.C., and reference librarian at the University of Central Florida Library in Orlando.

SANFORD BERMAN is Head Cataloger at Hennepin County Library in Minnesota. He is the author of *Prejudices and Antipathies: A Tract on the LC Subject Heads Concerning People* and *The Joy of Cataloging,* he is also well-known as an editor, and he contributes to professional journals.

MARJORIE E. BLOSS is Assistant Director for Technical Services and Automation at the Illinois Institute of Technology. She helped found the ALA/RTSD Committee on Union Lists of Serials and she serves on the OCLC Union List Standards Task Force, and the IFLA Section on Serial Publications.

DORIS HARGRETT CLACK is Professor in the School of Library and Information Studies at Florida State University in Tallahassee. Active in professional organizations, she is the author of numerous books and articles, including *The Making of a Code: Issues Underlying AACR2.*

JOHN P. COMAROMI is Editor and Chief of the Decimal Classification Division of the Library of Congress. He is a frequent contributor of books and articles to the professional literature. Among his books are *The Eighteen Editions of the Dewey Decimal Classification, Book Numbers,* and *Manual on the Use of the Dewey Decimal Classification: Edition 19.*

JEAN S. DECKER is Head of Serials Cataloging of the University Libraries at the State University of New York at Buffalo. She is active in professional organizations and a contributor to the literature of librarianship.

155

PAUL Z. DUBOIS is Director of the Trenton State College Library in New Jersey. Formerly he was Associate Director at the Kent State University Library. He is active in library organizations, a contributor to professional journals, and author of *Paul Leicester Ford, An American Man of Letters.*

ROSEMARY D. HARRICK is Head of the Reference Department at the Kent State University Library. She is active in professional organizations and was the coauthor, with Neal Edgar, of an article in *The Reference Librarian.*

BILL KATZ is a Professor in the School of Library and Information Science at the State University of New York at Albany. He is well known in the field as an educator, author and editor. Among his books are *Introduction to Reference Work, Collection Development, Magazines for Libraries,* and since 1970 he has edited *The Best of Library Literature.*

RUTH B. MCBRIDE is Central Circulation Librarian at the University of Illinois at Urbana where she formerly served as Serials/ Analytics Coordinator in the Automated Systems Department. She is an active participant in professional organizations and a frequent contributor to library literature.

BARBARA P. PINZELIK is General Services Librarian at the Purdue University Libraries in West Lafayette, Indiana. Active in professional organizations, she is also a contributor to professional journals.

A. ROBERT ROGERS is Dean of the School of Library Science at Kent State University, past President of the Ohio Library Association, and very active in professional organizations at both the national and state level. He is a frequent contributor to professional journals and he is the author of *The Humanities: A Selective Guide to Information Sources* and other books.

JAMES E. RUSH is President of his own library, computer and information science consulting firm, James E. Rush Associates, Inc. Before starting his consulting business, he was Director of Research for OCLC, Inc. He is a member of many professional organizations and a frequent contributor to professional journals. He is joint author of *A Guide to Information Science* and *Information Retrieval and Documentation in Chemistry.*

JEAN ACKER WRIGHT is Research and Development Librarian for General Technical Services at Vanderbilt University Library in Nashville. She has had a wide range of experience at Vanderbilt and, before that, at the Nashville Public Library and at the Tennessee State Library and Archives.